Thomas Gunn Selby

The Ministry of the Lord Jesus

Thomas Gunn Selby

The Ministry of the Lord Jesus

ISBN/EAN: 9783743347632

Manufactured in Europe, USA, Canada, Australia, Japa

Cover: Foto ©ninafisch / pixelio.de

Manufactured and distributed by brebook publishing software (www.brebook.com)

Thomas Gunn Selby

The Ministry of the Lord Jesus

BOOKS FOR BIBLE STUDENTS

Edited by the
REV. ARTHUR E. GREGORY.

THE MINISTRY OF THE LORD JESUS

BY

THOMAS G. SELBY.

London:
CHARLES H. KELLY,
2, CASTLE ST., CITY RD.; AND 66, PATERNOSTER ROW, E.C.
1896.

BOOKS FOR BIBLE STUDENTS.

Editor: REV. ARTHUR E. GREGORY.

The Epistles of Paul the Apostle. A Sketch of their Origin and Contents. By GEORGE G. FINDLAY, B.A. Small crown 8vo, 2s. 6d. Fifth Thousand.

The Theological Student. A Handbook of Elementary Theology. With List of Questions for Self-Examination. By J. ROBINSON GREGORY. 2s. 6d. Fifth Thousand.

The Gospel of John. An Exposition, with Critical Notes. By T. F. LOCKYER, B.A. 2s. 6d. Second Thousand.

The Praises of Israel. An Introduction to the Study of the Psalms. By W. T. DAVISON, M.A., D.D. 2s. 6d. Third Thousand.

The Wisdom-Literature of the Old Testament. By W. T. DAVISON, M.A., D.D. 2s. 6d. Second Thousand.

From Malachi to Matthew: Outlines of the History of Judea from 440 to 4 B.C. By Professor R. WADDY MOSS, Didsbury College, Manchester. 2s. 6d. Second Thousand.

An Introduction to the Study of Hebrew. By J. T. L. MAGGS, B.A., B.D., Prizeman in Hebrew and New Testament Greek, London University. 5s.

In the Apostolic Age: The Churches and the Doctrine. By ROBERT A. WATSON, M.A., D.D. 2s. 6d.

The Sweet Singer of Israel. Selected Psalms with Metrical Paraphrases. By BENJAMIN GREGORY, D.D. 2s. 6d.

The Age and Authorship of the Pentateuch. By WILLIAM SPIERS, M.A., F.G.S., etc. 3s. 6d.

A Manual of Modern Church History. By Professor W. F. SLATER, M.A. 2s. 6d.

An Introduction to the Study of New Testament Greek. By J. HOPE MOULTON, M.A., late Fellow of King's College, Cambridge. 3s.

The Ministry of the Lord Jesus. By T. G. SELBY. 2s. 6d.

The Divine Parable of History. An Exposition of the Revelation of St. John. By HENRY ARTHUR SMITH, M.A. 2s. 6d.

The Books of the Prophets. By GEORGE G. FINDLAY, B.A. Vol. I. to the Fall of Samaria. 2s. 6d.

WILL SHORTLY BE PUBLISHED.

A First Reader in New Testament Greek. By J. HOPE MOULTON, M.A.

The Evidences of Christianity. By Professor J. SHAW BANKS.

LONDON: CHARLES H. KELLY 2, CASTLE ST., CITY RD., E.C.
Dec. 1895.

THE MINISTRY

OF

THE LORD JESUS

BY

THOMAS G. SELBY,

AUTHOR OF "THE IMPERFECT ANGEL," ETC.

London:

CHARLES H. KELLY,

2, CASTLE ST., CITY RD.; AND 66, PATERNOSTER ROW, E.C.

1896.

CONTENTS

CHAP.		PAGE
I.	THE MANNER AND METHOD OF THE TEACHER	1
II.	THE SPRINGS OF AUTHORITY	18
III.	THE TEACHER VINDICATED BY HIS HUMILITY	37
IV.	THE MORAL PREPARATION FOR FAITH	56
V.	HUMAN FREEDOM AND DIVINE POWER	69
VI.	THE RACIAL LIMITATIONS OF THE MINISTRY	86
VII.	THE UNIVERSAL NOTE IN CHRIST'S TEACHING	101
VIII.	COUNSELS AGAINST WORLDLY CARE	120
IX.	THE SOWER AND THE GALILEAN OUTLOOK	137
X.	THE SEED AND THE MYSTERY OF ITS GROWTH	159
XI.	CHRIST'S VIEW OF THE SCRIPTURES	180
XII.	LEGAL AND EVANGELICAL GREATNESS	198
XIII.	OUR LORD'S IDEAL OF PRAYER	215
XIV.	THE PRAYER OF PATIENT STRUGGLE	229
XV.	CHRIST'S TEACHING ABOUT HIS OWN DEATH	240
XVI.	CHRIST'S TEACHING ABOUT HEAVEN	260
XVII.	CHRIST'S VIEW OF RETRIBUTION	279
XVIII.	THE SENSITIVENESS OF THE TEACHER TO HIS ENVIRONMENT	301

THE MINISTRY OF THE LORD JESUS.

CHAPTER I.

THE MANNER AND METHOD OF THE TEACHER.

HOW did the Prophet from the workshop at Nazareth carry Himself before the hearers who were attracted by His fame? What impression would His style have made upon us if we could have forgotten for a moment the substance of His message, and have turned our attention upon the mere accidents of His address? How would the modern pressman, who describes from the Reporters' Gallery of the House of Commons every gesture and accent of our political debaters, have pictured the art of this Teacher? The manner was so simple, so free from effort and artifice, so marked by the quiet and rhythmic spontaneity of perfect nature, that a modern critic would have found little to picture, and nothing to caricature. It had the charm of unaffected sincerity, and it is a somewhat remarkable thing that, although our Lord often had to speak to men of captious temper, and provoked the most venomous epithets by His plain dealing with the ruling classes of His time, no animadversion is ever cast upon His style. He succeeded at least in fixing the attention of friends and foes alike upon those principles which were the very heart of His message. If there had been the slightest suspicion of grotesqueness and sensationalism in His manner, some of the hostile criticisms He had to face would have worn a different complexion.

Where no question of conscience was at stake, the Great Teacher followed the methods current amongst His own countrymen, and was far too sane to make Himself gratuitously eccentric. Like the rabbi in his school, He sat in the midst of the Twelve as well as when addressing wider circles of hearers. His most formal and elaborate discourse, the Sermon on the Mount, as well as the Judgement Prophecy on the western slope of Olivet, was delivered in this attitude. He reclined at the banquets, and many of His most memorable sayings and parables group themselves under our modern phrase "table talk." When He unfolded the present and coming fortunes of His kingdom in those incomparable similitudes which succeed each other like the scenes in some historic tapestry, He sat in the boat, whilst the crowd spread itself out on the shore. After standing up to read in the synagogue at Nazareth, He sat down, before giving His own application of the stupendous prophecy. When arrested with a show of ruthless force which might have befitted the capture of a brigand or an insurrectionist, He says in His remonstrance, "I sat daily teaching in the temple." The attitude was not that of a fighter or a blatant incendiary given to gesticulation and setting himself to stir up the passions of the crowd. He placed Himself side by side with His hearers as though He were one of themselves, wishing to appeal to them in their quiet and self-collected moods, and bring them to due sobriety of thought and life. He was no stormy declaimer, and never ventured near the verge of mere harangue.

And yet His manner was by no means still and inanimate. When interrupted by a messenger from His family as He was teaching in the house at Capernaum, He turned to His disciples, and, stretching forth His hand, said,

"Behold My mother and My brethren." In applying His parable in the house of Simon the Pharisee, He turned with a glance of reproachful love to His supercilious host. He "looked round about" upon a captious and hostile audience, being grieved because of the hardness of their hearts. The slowness of His disciples to understand once compelled Him to enter upon the dramatic experiment of setting a little child in the midst of the Twelve, and making the child His text. As He was sitting in one of the courts of the temple at the Feast of Tabernacles, He suddenly rose to His feet and "cried." That was His rare method of emphasising or underlining a communication of paramount importance, and seems to have been but twice employed. It was an act of homage to the great Spirit who was to carry on His work, and of that Spirit He thereby made Himself herald and forerunner. The act marked a momentous turning-point in the history of His kingdom. In one of His last admonitory discourses in Jerusalem, He once again adopted this rare method of emphasising His message. And Jesus cried and said, "He that believeth on Me believeth not on Me but on Him that sent Me."

Not more than half a dozen of His recorded discourses are systematic and closely articulated.

He was accustomed to wait for the suggestion of the moment, and His instincts and inspirations were never at fault. In the fullest possible sense He achieved the ideal implied in the apostolic phrase, and was "always ready for every good word and work." The multitudes did not come together by prearrangement to listen to an hour's lecture, or a two-hours' political speech. At one stage in His ministry the renown of His miracles insured Him congregations which must have taxed His physical strength to the utmost; but as often as not He had to seek His hearers. He met them in their devout moods in the synagogues, in their social moods at private feasts, in their leisured moods by the wayside, in their expectant moods at the religious fairs of the capital, in their confidential moods during the quiet companionship of travel. He availed Himself of every opening in conversation which indicated the interest and religious accessibility of His hearers. Perhaps more often than not He waited for others to give Him His cue. He was always at home with the highest and most essential truth, and when He had to speak of the deep things of God no sense of constraint ever hampered Him.

He sought to fulfil the work of His brief life neither as a politician of constructive genius nor as a philosopher seeking by public disputation to sharpen the wits of His contemporaries, whilst at the same time He defined and developed His own half-formed views. Never setting Himself against the scholarly, or rudely repelling the learned, He yet addressed Himself expressly to the questions which were vital for the multitude. Jesus expected to find His absorbing sphere of activity in the common crowd, and in men chosen from the crowd, to whom He afterwards devoted Himself with special care, that they might at last go back and carry on their appointed tasks amongst those from whom they had been called. It was His one aim to work ever by moral influence and through direct contact with the rank and file of His fellow-countrymen. He had a message rather than a policy for which He was soliciting patronage and adoption, and He left the after-policy of His kingdom to be determined in due time by the genius of His message.

We cannot help comparing our Lord's method with that of other teachers who have influenced large sections of the human race. The sage of the Far East, whose name is a synonym of so much that is wholesome and excellent in social morality, was a compound of stipendiary magistrate and of privy councillor, and Confucianism is the apotheosis of that unpoetical combination. For the greater part of his life this worthy sage and patriot was looking round in the hope that some one of the feudal kings of ancient China would give him a chance, and commission him to play the part of an ethical Bismarck. He gathered disciples, whom he indoctrinated with his ideas of filial piety and statecraft, but this part of the work was intended to be a mere parenthesis in his programme, although the parenthesis at last outgrew the original scheme. It was an axiom with this ancient worthy that men would be moulded by the hand that governed them. "The people may be made to follow a plan of action, but not to understand it." "The rulers are like the wind, and the people like grass bending to the influence of their behests." It scarcely occurred to Confucius that an appeal to the popular conscience might achieve a reformation of manners, and he and his successors alike were paralysed by the assumption that the classes at the bottom of the social scale were unimprovable. They would have been aghast at our Lord's idea of finding amongst the base residuum the regenerating forces of the world. Confucius never thought of them as God's lost children, and no voice of authority came to him bidding him gather them home. He had his tribulations and disappointments, but these were trifles compared to those of Jesus Christ, and he died with the shadow of a deep despair for the fortunes of his race darkening his outlook. In spite of His sober insight and His unique experience of the shamefullest side of human life, Jesus lived a persistent optimist, and a martyr optimist He died.

This Prophet of Galilee had not, like another great teacher of the human race, to retire into the jungle to discover something. The sight of leprosy, indigence, death, did not shock Him into temporary catalepsy. He had reckoned with these things beforehand, and with the tragic moral facts at their root. His message was in Him, growing with His growth and expanding with His manhood, and He was ready for His vocation as soon as the door of the workshop at Nazareth had been finally closed. Attempts have been made to bracket our Lord's temptations in the wilderness with the sins which assailed Buddha in his seclusion, before he had won the secret of perfect rest; and the two stories are often pronounced variants of one primitive tradition. It was not, however, like Gautama Buddha, as a searcher after truth, that our Lord came into the wilderness, but rather that His loyalty to what He already knew might be tested and approved. The discipline of His own mystic life was never allowed to curtail His work for the multitude, nor did He impose seclusion and asceticism upon those who placed themselves under His control. He felt that what men needed was, not to be shut off like so many victims of mental disease in an asylum, and put under some strict regimen, but to be brought into contact with Himself and His message of hope and invigoration. He sought men wherever they could be found, and tried to gain their hearing for His helpful and saving words.

To the common conscience enlightened by the Scriptures, and acting in concert with a true judgement and affections, this new Prophet makes His appeals. He was more than once twitted with maintaining a reserve which kept men in suspense. The Jews wanted categorical answers to their questions, and those answers He did not choose to give, for the simple reason that it was a part of the process of moral salvation that every man should weigh and determine for himself. His reply was, that all material evidence was before them, and they must form their own conclusions. That was what He was ever urging men to do. In the process of domesticating men within His fold, Jesus did not mean to neglect and obscure and destroy the most sagacious instincts and faculties of the mind. To discern for themselves was no unimportant step in their training for salvation. It would have been an unworthy view of the ends of His own vocation if He had depreciated and put into the background man's capacity for forming intelligent and trustworthy moral judgements.

The message which is the roll-call of His opening ministry, "Repent, for the kingdom of heaven is at hand," aims at both awakening and cheering the conscience. It is the same deep, sacred, sensitive centre of life which Jesus touches alike in His conversation with Nicodemus and in the discourse by the well. The fact that a scrupulous city scholar should have overlooked the most essential promise of the covenant, and forgotten the need of the new birth, was the sign of a distorted ethic beneath this faultless exterior. Before healing the malady of nerves and sinews, Jesus pacified the haunted conscience of the man who was sick of palsy. In the Sermon on the Mount He seeks to give to the shrivelled moral sense of the Jew a wider range of activity and obligation. The conscience which had hitherto been parochial, He makes catholic and cosmopolitan. By an appeal to this same moral faculty, He could silence adversaries who might seem to be imperturbable as the brass of the Temple gates, and bring back the long-lost blush of shame to their cheeks. He had faith in its witness under the most corrupt conditions of society, and counted it as an ally which would never fail.

And there was also a conscience of the sentiments and affections to which our Lord made His appeal, certain that a right response would be given. In His Sabbath controversies and in His talks upon the casuistry of ritual, He turns boldly from the conventions of a degenerate age to the ever fresh and responsive instinct of kindness in the heart of humanity. It is to the intuitive benignity of the heart He speaks at the feast of Levi, and He shows that the voice of sympathy and compassion in the human breast is one with the voice of God in the Scriptures. When the Jews press around Him in the Temple courts, as well as when confronted with the question set by the messengers of the imprisoned Baptist, He points to His works as an adequate certificate of His office. He is not calling attention only to the supernatural qualities of those works, but to the essential grace and compassion by which they are distinguished. He commends childlikeness, He declares the

Divine Fatherhood, He speaks of the prodigal and his home welcome, and in so doing He makes the best instincts of the family-life second His message. But at the same time He is careful to show that all that is sacred in man is there, not as a gift of nature, but by the grace and inward activity of the Father. He approves the faith so mysteriously begotten in the heart of the centurion, and lets it speak for the instruction of others. He declares that Simon's confession of his Master's superhuman personality is the fruit of an inward revelation. He wrought as a teacher to bring into view the Divine activities which were in process in the souls of men; and in these facts to which He directed the attention of His followers He found the starting-point for His own teaching about the work and ministry of the Comforter.

And these appeals to the conscience and affections as organs of God's immanent activity are carried out upon the lines of a strictly logical method. He gives due recognition to the personal judgements of His hearers, and never arbitrarily imposes His own dogmas upon strangers. He speaks to a reason in men which inevitably condemns the low cunning and pride and spitefulness of their baser prejudices. "If Satan cast out Satan, how can his kingdom stand?" He tries to awaken in men powers by which they may discern truth for themselves, or at least its more obvious elements. "How doth David call Him Lord?" Men must search out the key to the paradox. "The baptism of John, was it from heaven or of men?" The answer must not be ignobly or irresolutely shirked. If men want to hang the question up for a time, they must be made to feel in the attempt what timid time-servers they are. Simon the Pharisee must share the speaker's argument, as the parable of the greater and the less forgiveness unfolds itself, and must intelligently commit himself to the great conclusion before it is expressly stated. By all His teaching Jesus seeks to direct men in their thinkings, rather than to think in their stead and impose the sum of His results upon their dull and slavish souls.

Weariness never checks the flow of His message. Wrangling, mortification, and that superficial success which is sometimes more distressing than failure, did not sicken Him of His work. No impoliteness or affront ever disturbed the serenity of His discourse or brought a jarring note into its strains. He lived for months in an atmosphere of captious criticism and contentiousness, but it did not embitter His temper, or breed uncertainty in His own mind about the worth and genuineness of His message. Argument mixed with vituperation did not heat His blood, or cause Him to forget that He was a herald of good tidings. Internecine strife between the disciples failed to chill His zeal. Criticisms, discourtesies, bad manners, disputations, often gave Him an impressive text. He went about to find on what side human nature was most open to His appeals. The receptivity of His congregation was His first study rather than the art of setting out those immeasurable reserves of wisdom and knowledge He had brought into human life.

In the Memoirs of Confucius it is said that the sage made it a rule never to repeat a lesson. The statement is not intended as a note of his versatility, but rather as a hint of the exacting rules laid down to secure attention from his disciples. The method had its advantages from the schoolmaster's standpoint, although it was somewhat harsh and supercilious. Much recent criticism on the Gospels implies that Jesus is entitled to the same dubious compliment. Whenever the Evangelists place any of our Lord's sayings in different localities and associations, it is assumed that they are drawing from one common fund of tradition, and guessing at the setting of circumstances into which the saying is fitted. Matthew, in his version of the Sermon on the Mount, is said to have systematised many of our Lord's disconnected sayings, and brought them into some kind of logical order and association. Luke borrowed the charge given to the Twelve, and put it, with certain modifications, into our Lord's lips when He was sending forth the Seventy. Luke's version of the Prodigal Son and his churlish brother is an elaboration of the parable given in Matthew about the Two Sons. The Pounds and the Talents are diversified survivals of one original parable. The parable of the Lost Sheep and the seeking shepherd, which belongs to the Perean ministry, is inserted by Matthew in the heart of the discourse about "the little ones."

The question, "Did Jesus repeat His discourses?" has a vital bearing upon the degree of trustworthiness attaching to the Gospel records. The present writer is not disposed to attempt so much in the way of harmonising as in his earlier studies, nor does he account it necessary to an orthodox theory of inspiration that each of the four Evangelists should know the exact date, place, and circumstance under which some particular saying of our Lord was uttered. But at the same time he cannot for a moment think that in the synoptical Gospels we have successive transformations of one primitive tradition only, and the assumption behind recent redactionist theories of the Gospels, that Jesus never repeated a saying or discourse, with the changes necessary to adapt it to a new audience, is out of harmony with all true conceptions of the character and personality of Jesus.

In different parts of the country the Great Teacher must have met people in practically the same conditions of mind and moral feeling, and might well repeat, with suitable modifications, parables and sayings used elsewhere. He was an itinerant evangelist, and surely could be allowed to touch chords touched with impressive effect in other districts. What was best for one gathering of men on a certain level of preparation for His message might be best for others on a similar level. The same people might well need a reiteration of lessons already given. The disciples themselves had to have the same facts drilled into them again and again, and what was needful in their case may have been much more needful with those who were less awake to the significance of our Lord's spirit and doctrine.

To assume that our Lord never repeats a saying makes the motive of His ministry too entirely intellectual. He was not concerned to display His versatility and inventiveness. Such theories of our Lord's ministry attribute to Him the pride and ambition of a French *chef*, who would feel himself under a shadow if he could not concoct something entirely new and artistic every time he is put upon his mettle by the presence of guests. When our Lord opened His lips, He thought more of His hearers and their needs than of setting forth His own splendid variety of resource. Our view of the character of Jesus is radically mistaken if He always aimed at saying something He had never said before. The force of His message was not dependent upon the novelty of its intellectual form. To exclude repetition from the ministry of our Lord is to banish moral and religious in favour of literary motives. Had He not set Himself to instruct and to save men rather than to dazzle His hearers with the flash of the unexpected in phrase and similitude? In the Jesus of the Gospels there is no taint of rhetorical pride, and to avoid traversing the same truth a second time, or enforcing a much-needed lesson by the same figure or allegory, implies an overweening fastidiousness and an intellectual detachment quite foreign to the meek and lowly Prophet of Nazareth.

CHAPTER II.

THE SPRINGS OF AUTHORITY.

ALTHOUGH the same Greek word is variously translated "power" and "authority" in both the Authorised and the Revised Versions of the New Testament, authority may exist without power; and the highest forms of power may exist without that formal investiture which those trained in official traditions are accustomed to associate with the word authority. Authority is sometimes inherent in the natural relationships which exist between man and man. At other times it is delegated and conferred by rite and symbol. And yet again it insensibly accrues to a man through his life-long growth in learning, wisdom, experience, virtue. Authority may be momentary, or it may be eternal. It may rest upon sure and certain right, or it may be usurped. On the Mount of Temptation, Satan offered to Jesus authority over the enchanted kingdoms arrayed before His view. Such authority had been surreptitiously arrogated, and the vaunted assertion of it was the short-lived lie of an impostor.

The Evangelists ascribe authority to our Lord in the domain of nature, over the thrones, dominions, principalities of the spirit world,— good and bad alike submitting to His sway, and in the realms of reason and intelligence. His command over the forces of nature, and His power to compel obedience amongst the legions of the air, was one and the same in its root and essence with His authority in the realm of ideas. He was commissioned and effectually qualified to enforce truth upon the conscience of mankind. Authority is not always able to press home its claims and to achieve its ends. It has reached its supreme embodiment when, in face of man's base, riotous passions, it can vindicate what is best and most sacred, and effectually bind the law of absolute right upon the conscience. All forms of human authority stop short at this point. As healer, absolver, teacher of men, Jesus never failed to make bystanders feel His transcendent power. Whether on the mountain side, in the private home, or in the thronged synagogue, this was the one thing men felt about His teaching, that, unlike the disquisitions of the scribes, it had the emphatic and unmistakable note of authority. He made the writ of the Eternal run in the most lawless and demoralised sections of society.

In their day the scribes had rendered to the cause of religion service of no mean value; but their day was gone. They were now like aborted organs in the body politic, once fulfilling useful and necessary functions, but interesting in the end of the dispensation only as vestiges of a departed past. For generations they had popularised the language of the law and the prophets, but had now reached the dotage of mere professionalism.

The scribes could glory in some of those accidents of authority which our Lord entirely lacked; and our Lord, of course, had those essential qualities of genuine living authority of which scarcely a trace could be found in the character and teaching of a typical scribe.

The scribes could boast that their authority, such as it was, rested upon a basis that was unimpeachably historic. They were the lineal representatives of those who had been educated in the schools of the prophets, and counted with much pride each link in the chain of their succession. From the Captivity downwards they had been found in every town and city of the land; for, as the speech of the primitive Jews had been repeatedly modified through intercourse with foreign nations, the service of these quondam interpreters became almost indispensable. The order was historic, and on this ground claimed and commanded no little respect from the masses; for then, as now with many minds, high antiquity and authority in all matters of religious faith are interchangeable terms. Under such a test Jesus Christ must have been relegated to a lower category than the scribes. He represented what was new, and in the judgement of contemporary ecclesiastics was an upstart, whilst his rivals represented an order which was old, and, alas! ineffectual. Our Lord inherited no credentials, but had to create them by the temper and the fruits of His own ministry. He could look to no line of predecessors. In His prophetic as well as in His priestly office He lacked the prestige of an elaborate genealogy, being "without father or mother," and leaving behind no formally designated heir.

If authority is to be measured in terms of technical scholarship, the scribes held the vantage ground. It must not be assumed that the Carpenter-Prophet was rude and unlettered, for He had a working knowledge of three languages. He had passed through the primary schools of His adopted town, and may possibly have read from night to night in the library of the synagogue at Nazareth, but He had not enjoyed what, in modern speech, would be called a university training. He had never sat at the feet of the great rabbis in Jerusalem, although He proved Himself once and again, in the very citadel of learning itself, more than a match for its most accomplished experts. In the mere letter of the classical scriptures He was not such an adept as the scribes, nor could He have made Himself so without grave mental and spiritual loss. It is inconceivable that this holy youth, with the prescience of a redemptive mission upon His conscience, should have spent days and nights in hair-splitting philologies and loud-swelling debates about tithes and lustrations, dress and ritual. The professional education of these scribes had been carried to a far more elaborate point than that of the carpenter's son. Indeed, its effect had been to make them blind to vital principles and infatuated with the mere letter of the word. In respect to those technical accomplishments on which colleges put their hall-mark, the scribe had every advantage over the artisan rabbi.

State officialism was on the side of the scribes, and conferred upon them just as much authority as it was able to bestow. The scribes, who were scholars by profession rather than sectaries, fraternised with both Pharisees and Sadducees, although, perhaps, their own special pursuits led them to sympathise with the policy of the former rather than of the latter party. They were a power to be reckoned with, and from all sides they received countenance, favour, support. Probably they were licensed for their calling, and were a recognised part of the theocracy of the latter days. Public honours were heaped upon them. No civil function would have been complete without their presence. They filled the chief seats at state banquets, never being compelled to sit, like the English clergy of the Middle Ages, cheek by jowl with clowns and court barbers. And the power conferred upon them by the chiefs of the dominant parties they used without restraint or reserve. It has been thought by some students of the life and times of the Messiah, that Jesus had been formally licensed to teach by one of the sects of the Essenes or He would not have been allowed to read and exhort in the synagogues. But for that hypothesis there is not the shred of an argument. He had no claim to address His fellow-townsmen but that of His own character. The temporal power was with the scribes and against the strolling Carpenter. And yet, in the eyes of plain, discerning people, they had less authority than the unfashionable Prophet who was hunted by the rulers of the earth in the time of His infancy, and thereafter was never beholden for a single advantage to the patronage of the classes.

Fashion bowed to the authority of the scribes, and consistently set itself to maintain their influence. To spurn a publican and fawn upon a scribe was an elementary etiquette of those times. The counsel of this favoured order was sought upon all critical occasions, and nothing more remained to be said after they had once spoken. The dominion of fashion in common things is a curious phenomenon, but its influence over religion is one of those first-class anomalies few people try to explain. Fashion did nothing for Jesus whilst He was alive but take His judgement away by the voices of its representatives in the Sanhedrim, and has never subsequently repaired to the kingdom founded in His innocent blood the wrong it wrought upon His person. But it did everything for the scribes. It pampered them, smoothed their pathways, buttressed their influence, cried up their knowledge and piety, extolled their names, and at the same time destroyed the pith of their manliness. "They that wear soft clothing are in kings' houses."

But when fashion had done its best on their behalf, the common judgement held them to be men of straw, and detected the hollowness of their message. Men instinctively felt that they lacked authority in its inmost essence, whilst the unfashionable Teacher, who had no other advantages on His side than those which were purely spiritual, spoke with an imperial force distinct from that of all other voices of the age. The maximum degree of earthly prestige and prerogative could not create the first rudiments of authority. The teaching of these pragmatists lacked the note of power, penetration, genuineness; and no adventitious rank could atone for the defect. The poor message they chattered was neutralised by pedantry, partisanships, frivolous casuistries, dead-level platitudes. The more they wrought, the more the channels of deep saving truth seemed to silt up and choke. There was room for a teacher of transcendent power and with a message straight from heaven, if one such could be found.

Into the authority exerted by our Lord over His hearers, no artifice or strain of self-assumption entered. He did not publicly announce His superhuman antecedents, and till the very close of His ministry rested nothing whatever upon His descent from David. His ministry He opened without induction service. He assumed no distinctive dress, nor did it ever occur to Him that He should read Himself in. He prefixed no apology or preamble to His sermons. The influence of His teaching and personality He allowed to silently permeate the mind of the multitude, just as the sunlight quietly sinks into growing herb and unfolding flower of the field. He left His origin a mystery, rightly judging that His authority would prove itself by the truth He taught and lived, rather than that the truth would be proved by His authority. Like the august solemnities of nature, He silently pervaded men's hearts and lives. Authority often reaches its most impressive enthronement where the verbal profession of it is scrupulously kept in the background. The master-sign by which we are led to expect the presence of transcendent power is humility. The assumption of the man who makes an open boast of his office always leads onlookers to think that it is a charlatan and an impostor who solicits their suffrages. Our Lord's office and personality at the outset were to be inferred rather than proclaimed, and this reticence was maintained, not only because of the stress of the times, but as the spontaneous fruit of His own lowliness. He left men to find out who He was by the manner of

His life and doctrine, and if that did not commend Him to their loyalty and reverent love, He was content for the time being to pass unrecognised. Reversing all ecclesiastical precedents and processes, He demonstrated the greatness of His office by the intrinsic quality of His work and teaching.

What were the essential constituents of that authority possessed by the Carpenter, but lacking in the ministrations of the scribes?

Men felt that His at least was the supreme prerogative which belongs to love. In strict equity, the one who loves best has the largest right of command, and in every age and place that principle is instinctively recognised. It is to some such principle the Master traces back His sovereign rights over the disciples in His allegory of the Good Shepherd. "The good shepherd layeth down his life for the sheep." In that declaration our Lord was just as true to the philosophy of history as to the first elements of religion. Authority has grown from the seed of love, however little sometimes it may have bred true to its beginnings. The earliest form of authority in the world was that of the parent over his offspring. At the next step we find the parent and his lineal representative clothed with power over the group of families springing from the primitive family. The State is simply the clan many times magnified, and the ruler of the State is the successor to the patriarch of the clan, and so there is a core of sociological truth in the Chinese saying, that "The emperor is father and mother of his people." No one seriously disputes the authority of love; and when the anarchist, who is sometimes a demented patriot, sets himself to overturn the State, it is for the simple reason that in his judgement the State no longer embodies the regal instinct of parental tenderness. The deepest root of authority is goodness. No impartial student can read through the Sermon on the Mount without being made to feel how profoundly the Galilean Preacher loves men, and what high sanction His word borrows from that fact. Much that He says is stern and searching, but it searches like the surgeon's probe, and not like the poisoned barb of one who has set himself to vilify and defame our common human nature. The Preacher wants to touch man's deepest disease and to heal his bitterest and most rankling grief, nor will He consent to gloss over insidious ailments, in the temper of a professional flatterer. What high ideals of spirit and conduct He sets up for men,—ideals which an average moralist would rate as extravagant! Is that no sign of love? The one to whom we are dearest always cherishes the loftiest vision of our future. Those who have no interest in us, mere speaking acquaintances, the observers who contemplate us from the other side of the street, do not expect us to do great things or lay down high codes for our observance. Jesus puts supreme excellence before the multitude, and aims at stimulating one and all to its undaunted pursuit. In His solicitude for men's best welfare He points out a royal road of escape from care, so that they may be free to grow spiritual. Unlike the scribes, who bound upon men burdens they would not touch with one of their fingers, He seeks to unloose the loads which crush the best thoughts and instincts of the human heart and to let the oppressed go free, taking upon Himself the sum of their grief and care.

The Sermon on the Mount is sometimes spoken of as though it were purely ethical, but from the beginning there is the earnest of sacrifice in it, and one feels the Speaker would gladly die to make men perfect and raise them to those spiritual excellencies He so fondly portrays. This indisputable authority, of which the multitude was so vividly sensible, has its deepest spring in the grand passion of love which throbs throughout the discourse.

Another element in all valid and commanding authority is knowledge. Whilst the sanction of rule rests upon love, that love must operate through discernment, sagacity, foresight. In ninety-nine cases out of a hundred the authority of a parent over the child is recognised and upheld; in the hundredth case there may be such defect and deficiency of intellectual power that natural rights and prerogatives must be set aside, and the State must create some new authority for the direction of a child's training and the safeguarding of his interests. The title to command, even when founded in nature, may be invalidated through mental disease and incapacity, just as the insanity of a king may compel the appointment of a regency. The authority of love must be linked with knowledge which is broad, deep, high. The Divine Teacher has matchless insight into human character, and equally matchless insight into the significance of right and wrong in that eternal realm of which man is a part. How rare it is to find these two things meet in the same mind! The man who looks into eternity seems to know but little of human character; and the man who knows human nature through and through is, or has been, a man of the world in a somewhat uncomplimentary sense. The marvellous thing about

Jesus Christ was that He should have known the secrets of two worlds with equal lucidity; and it is that fact which gives unique power to His ministry.

The eye which is that of authority must always search beneath the surface of human life, and no one can study the Sermon on the Mount without being made to feel that Jesus reads men deeply. A hakeem is called in to see one who is sick, and, having no knowledge of physiology and its kindred sciences, he professes to ascertain the disease and to work out a method of cure by taking note of the positions of the planets at the time of his patient's seizure. A scientific doctor is able to locate every organ, and to correctly interpret the complex symptoms of derangement. The scribes did their work by a method as wide of the mark as the first, and Jesus Christ by a process more full of certainty even than the second. He detects every step of man's malady, putting His finger upon the successive stages of its devastating progress through the soul. The scribes owed whatever popularity they had to the fact that they never went below the surface of human nature, and systematically ignored in their teachings the heinousness attaching to inward delinquencies. Jesus, though in no superficial sense popular with

His hearers, made them sensible of His sovereignty, because He looked them through with the inevitableness and flashing surprise of an electric search-light. The eye which reads the secret pride in the souls of conspicuous pietists is the eye of an authority which is not only royal but also divine. However much men may be tempted to evade the truth, they are compelled to confess that the gaze of supernatural judgement is looking down upon them. One of the enigmas which those who treat Jesus as though He were man, and only man, have to reckon with is, that this sinless One knew more of the insidiousness, secret pain, far-reaching ramifications of the mystery of sin than the sinner himself. He carries the keys and moves at will through the mazes of human guilt and self-deception, and yet moves, not as a spy, but as a healer of incomparable skill.

As Jesus speaks, the impression grows apace that He is at home in the realms of the invisible; for He insists as much on inward as on outward purity. He makes little of rites, but much of that inward sanctification to which rites in their original design pointed. The scribes may be compared to a sweep and charwoman who have blundered at the wrong hour into the shop and workroom of the chronometer-maker. Hair-fine movements, gossamer mechanisms, delicate tools lie exposed on every side, whilst the sweep brings small avalanches of soot down the chimney, and the charwoman follows in his steps, dusting tables, beating cushions, sweeping floors. They are making clean that which is without, not thinking of the mischief done by their short-sighted efforts. The open chronometers, the jewelled movements and delicate balance-wheels, and springs slender as floss silk, will be choked and clogged and impaired by this ignorant bustle and fuss. When the man in authority appears upon the scene, he will soon stop these mistimed sweepings and furbishments. He does not look upon the world as a heap of little townships with chimneys to be swept, rooms to be cleaned, and chairs to be dusted. He has to think of that more delicate side of scientific civilisation which sweep and office-cleaner unwittingly touch and imperil for a time. He occupies an entirely different standpoint, and remembers the lives and fortunes depending upon the exact measurement of time, and the enlarged possibilities of knowledge to which the minute mechanisms ignored by these unskilled blunderers are contributory. The scribes saw things from petty, provincial, momentary standpoints, and made one of the chief ends of life the mere cleansing of cups and platters and the decoration of the surface of society. Jesus Christ saw things in their infinite and eternal ranges, and insisted upon a scrupulous, delicate inward righteousness which should fit the enduring verities of being ; and the sense of eternal relationships asserts itself through His speech and clothes His mission with authority. In seeking to cleanse the conscience, in applying His law to the remotest labyrinths of conduct, in demanding sincerities which would bear the light of God's closest examination, our Lord not only proved His mastery over the facts of human character, but His insight into the substance of those demands which the eternal world was even now making upon men.

This impression of authority culminated in the unformulated conviction of the multitudes, that one who could so speak must enjoy an intimate participation in the Divine character and counsels not possessed by the holiest prophet of the past. He made the truth live, and live with stupendous pulsations,—and that not by the mere craft of the dramatist, for He taught out of strange and comprehensive experiences. He had obviously seen right and wrong tested in wider fields and upon scales of vaster time-measurement than His contemporaries. Must not such an one, before His sojourn amongst men, have moved in realms of life and consciousness where offences of mind were regarded as gravely as delinquencies of outward act. An unspiritual functionary can never have authority, however long the line of his predecessors or however many the honours heaped upon his office. No ordination or investiture can confer it. It can make him at best into a superior scribe, a mere foil to the Prophet of Nazareth. He to whom supreme authority is assigned must not only have that intense conviction which comes from gazing stedfastly into the realms of the spiritual, and taking in the root-facts and principles of the Divine judgements, but must himself have been an actor in this strange world. The voice on the Galilean hillside rang forth with the emphasis of eternity in its tone, and such discourse was impossible to one living only in the realms of sense. The speaker must have stood nearer than others to the throne of the Most High, and have drunk at the same sacred fount of thought. Hence was it that when He began to speak of His own part in a judgement to come, and to make Himself the mouthpiece of the last sentence of doom, " I never knew you: depart from Me, ye that work iniquity," there was no revolt provoked, and no sense of incongruity in the tacit claim. The voice of the prophet rises into the yet more majestic voice of the judge, and the multitudes begin to feel it is indeed the Supreme Arbiter of character and destiny who speaks to them. His authority transcends all human patterns, and His hearers confess that His word is soul-awakening as the trumpet-peal from Sinai, irresistible, almost, perhaps indeed altogether, Divine.

CHAPTER III.

THE TEACHER VINDICATED BY HIS HUMILITY.

IN morbid moods the temptation comes to us to doubt Christ's superhuman origin, or at least to hold our judgements in suspense, because He said so little regarding Himself and His preterhuman experience and history. He might surely have given us more specific information about His own wonderful person, and not have left all that to be said by others. He claimed to be the Son of God, and was sentenced to death because of the perilous inferences which, in the judgement of the Sanhedrim, were implicit in the claim; but He did not tell men definitely how far His relation to the Deity differed from that of those He was pleased to call His "brethren." Was the relation peculiar and distinctive, or was it common? When affirming His eternal sojourn in the bosom of the Father, He might surely have ventured to give His contemporaries and their successors a glimpse into the wonderful communications of which He had been the favoured recipient, and disclosed some of the mysteries learned in His position of unique privilege. He told His disciples little, and the world comparatively nothing, about His pre-human life. Why did He not vouchsafe ampler insight into His own part at the making of the universe and the place of transcendent honour He filled amongst the sons of light?

If such questions present difficulty, the Great Teacher Himself has anticipated the answer. To have dwelt upon such matters at length would have invalidated His credentials. "He that speaketh of himself seeketh his own glory." These reserves were the necessary outworking of His incomparable humility, and in a world seething with the ferment of rapacious ambition, freedom from the temper of self-exaltation is the most convincing token thoughtful men can have that His doctrine is not of Himself but from above. The self-anointed prophet, the self-separated priest, the self-elected messiah, is a man of egotism and phenomenal pride. God never speaks through the man who magnifies himself, but lifts to the most transcendent distinctions of service the man who puts himself into the dust. The self-interested and self-seeking person is discredited from the beginning. He has subsidiary aims, and cannot adequately know himself, much less what is outside and beyond him, whilst hot in the pursuit of those aims. If one absolutely free from ambition can be found, we may venture to put unlimited trust in his message.

Is the test valid? Are there not humble and self-renouncing men amongst us to whom God does not speak truth of any special import or value to the larger world? If such men there are, we shall never hear from their lips the complaint that God has left them without a message, for that very complaint would imply a confidence in their own fitness to be oracles quite inconsistent with genuine and heart-deep humility.

The test is one to which we are accustomed to attach slight importance, and that fact, if fairly looked at, may serve to assure us of its complete validity. It is not often we hear that Jesus is the very Word of God to us, inasmuch as He gave proof by both life and death of a humility without historical parallel. In His controversy with the Jews our Lord points again and again to the sign of humility, but, like the scribes and the Pharisees, we want other signs, and half assume that this method of proof is out of date and has no special relevancy in the present day. Perhaps one reason why we ignore it is that it would involve an impressive rebuke to our pride. We do not expect to find lofty privilege and majestic authority identified with a virtue we at least are not in the habit of putting in the forefront of our ethic. The very fact that we assign it a secondary place convicts us of vanity, and illustrates our stinted esteem for a character into which no strain of worldly ambition enters. What an inestimable and admonitory lesson it is for us to go to His feet and learn that the most incontestable token of His authority is this,—that He is lowly beyond all others and entirely self-renouncing! It is our imperfect apprehension of the guilt inherent in vanity and self-assertion which blinds us to this the most legible of His credentials. He has the ethical mark which classifies Him with a world the first principles of which are in sharp antithesis to the pomp and pretence of our own. His right to teach and His power to still the tumult of fear and passion is based upon the fact that He is "meek and lowly in heart."

If this test is demonstrably valid, and is applied with scrupulous care, it will make the task of choosing Him who is to be the guide and sovereign of our souls one of modest compass, for there are few men who strictly answer to the test. A natural instinct prompts us to desire the esteem and goodwill of those amongst whom we move, and not one man in a thousand knows where to draw the line and to decline that excess of respect which becomes adulation and idolatry. So that we can regale our hearts with the plaudits of approving friends, we are not particular about the stopping-point. We encourage, perhaps legitimately, a certain amount of ambition in the young; for we want to stir them up to succeed. Good men sometimes set themselves to win the notice of multitudes, professedly for the purpose of increasing their usefulness, although it does seem as though such strategy must keep them back from the highest excellencies of the Christian life and character. Those whose religious sincerity we should be sorry to challenge write themselves up in the newspapers, practise the tricks of log-rolling, use their public positions to retail with more or less of delicacy the sweet and flattering things which have been said about them. Egotism seems to be one of the least curable of the foibles of the flesh. The person who will impress us with his humility when we look at him from afar will appear in a somewhat different light when we come into his inner circle, and in moods of closeted confidence hear him tell many gratifying facts about himself at which we had been left to guess before. Reserved for a while about the estimate he entertains of his own power and achievement, all at once we find it has been very flattering, and he has heretofore been discreet rather than humble. And then, again, a man will seem singularly lowly and unpretending, and the more his friends accord to him the less will he be disposed to assume; but all at once he has to pass through an ordeal of glaring and unjust depreciation, and latent pride breaks out, and we are surprised to find how much he arrogates to himself. The trampled worm turns at last, and with all the haughty airs of a fiery dragon. The adept in statecraft will behave himself for a time like a weaned child, and then make a sudden dash for fame and power. The Divine Teacher's humility was uniform and lifelong.

The lowly ones of the earth are but a handful, and of these there is but one who has not been schooled into humility by the memory of sin. If we could pass through their ranks and apply the test our Lord gave to the Jews, "He that speaketh of himself seeketh his own glory," can we doubt who of them would be the man of our choice? "Should we not say, I will accept the one who is least inclined to exalt and magnify himself? The law of heaven shall be the rule of my faith; the highest throne to the one whose humility transcends the rest." It is from the midst of no bewildering multitude we have to pick our guide. A specific supernatural distinction rests upon him who is perfectly lowly; and one only of the characters of history wears this fleckless halo.

Under the normal conditions of life, a man who is indifferent to the world's praise or blame cannot fall into the temptation of accounting himself a prophet of God when he is not such. At the root of every form of religious pretence and hallucination there is a mood of vanity, and where subtle allurements of the type which were addressed to the Lord in the wilderness succeed, there must obviously be more or less of moral defect. No religious vagary is ever intellectual only. The student of physics tells us that clouds could not possibly form and poise themselves in the air above us, but for the fact that it is full of fine particles of matter to which the films of vapour cleave. And unless there are floating atoms of pride, egotism, self-esteem in the character, a man's view of Divine realities will not be overspread and obscured with phantasies and illusive imaginations. A passion for notoriety will sometimes lead men into the same obliquities as the grosser passions, which are the staple of commonplace crime; and when the unsent-prophet, the pseudo-messiah, the self-ordained leader appears upon the scene to rally a silly and rabble following, he is commonly a product of the same passion. The French rationalist insinuates that Jesus was led away from His native simplicity by the enthusiasms of the multitude, and at last came, consciously or unconsciously, to fit Himself into their conception of the ideal hero to whom they were ascribing superhuman prerogatives. The theory implies moral deterioration, and deterioration that must have taken its rise in a waning spirit of humility and self-renunciation. Of such a change, however, we can find no trace. Every temptation implies a motive on which it must fasten before it can effectuate itself, and it is a question whether the currents of thought in the brain would continue to move without the spur of an ethical or animal impulse. It is difficult to see how a mind free from pride and self-seeking can be moved by an inducement to assume unreal and abnormal prerogative. At some stage or other, the wish to magnify one's place in the universe must beget a palpable vanity before there can be religious imposture. It is quite inconceivable that a man should be the victim of a purely intellectual temptation, and lay claim for his work and message to an authority from God that after all is only spurious. The organisms which produce ferment and decay must have a medium in which to propagate themselves; and a false prophecy, an illusive vocation, a spurious embassage, all the things which give rise to the putridities of occult philosophy and heathen superstition, must operate through elements of vanity, ambition, self-worship lurking in the heart of the pretender.

Can we not conceive of circumstances under which a man completely humble in motive and conduct might fall into the mistake of thinking himself God-sent and God-inspired? Idiosyncrasy or mental disease does sometimes give rise to strange perturbations of the reason; and if we allow a possibility of that kind, is the logic quite conclusive?

Our Lord Himself seemed so dead to the motives actuating the average man, that some of His friends felt they could not judge Him by common rules, and in their perplexity suggested that He was beside Himself, so heedless was He of the things they coveted most. In a totally vicious world the sudden appearance of a virtue would be looked upon as a phase of insanity; and no wonder the friends of one so abnormally humble and unworldly should have thought Him ill-balanced, if not insane. It is perhaps rather surprising that more has not been made of that theory by modern unbelievers, as it is a less hopeless theory by which to explain the feats and movements of this wonderful personality than nine-tenths of the theories which have been devised. Strange illusions arise with any little brain disturbance, and in every county asylum there may be found a Prince of Wales, an Emperor William, two or three Messiahs, with an angel Gabriel to complete the circle. A recent book attempts to prove that genius is thinly-veiled insanity, and that the passing idols of European literature are neurotics. And a French realist sets himself to show, in a series of novels, that hereditary taint may assume drunkenness and nameless sensuality in one generation, phthisis in another, homicide in a third, and mystical and over-wrought piety in yet a fourth. It now remains for some profane scientist to fix the place of Jesus Christ in the order of the neurotics.

To all such irreverent theories it is a sufficient reply that insanity in its initiatory stages is rarely, if ever, associated with perfect humility. In fact, humility is an effectual safeguard of a man's sanity. There are, of course, instances in which the causes of mental disease are purely physical, but in the great majority of cases the sentiments and passions are predisposing causes. In the very process of being victimised by his own lusts, a man becomes an egotist, and intemperance and sensuality are self-assertions of the blood. The brain is sometimes unbalanced by disappointment, but disappointment implies pride, overstrained ambition, a sanguine and selfish outlook which has made of frustrated dreams a tragedy maiming the reason. Irrepressible egotism is the antecedent condition of insanity in the man who thinks himself a Rothschild, the Tsar of Russia, or the providential king of the restored Jews. Rarely, indeed, do humility and madness go together. Even religious melancholia itself is the product of morbid self-consciousness rather than of excessive humility. We can scarcely imagine of a man of perfect modesty falling into mental disease or being led away by the delusion that he has the afflatus of the prophet. This great Teacher is no overheated and proud enthusiast, but is calm, sagacious, sober-minded. He represses the sudden exhibition of feeling in the scribe who wishes to be a follower, and calls him to self-examination. He checks Peter's outbursts of chivalrous but self-misjudging heroism and sacrifice. To the woman in the crowd who cries, " Blessed is the womb that bare Thee, and the paps that gave Thee suck," He gives no rash and excitement-kindling answer, but declares the blessedness of all who hear and do the will of God. He is always quiet and lowly, and has that unmistakable humility which is at once the proof and preservative of man's sanity.

Is not pure and unmixed humility the miracle of the moral world, and does not the quality mark out its possessor as a channel of the highest spiritual communications? The desire men have to be looked up to by their fellows is inborn and world-wide. The heart craves for homage as instinctively as the senses seek sunshine, zephyrs, the rippling cadences of speech. He who is lifted above this weakness must have a being, the more sensitive half of which is played upon by influences travelling from beyond the confines of visible nature. A humility ruling the deepest and most intricate movements of the spirit must be God-wrought in its beginnings. If one come to us whose nature is sweet and tender as the dew, and who at the same time seeks no glory for himself, we can accept him as a sign in the kingdom of Divine ideas. He is like a new-made star in the firmament, with all the lustre of its fresh birth still clinging to it, and is obviously invested for a great embassy. God is always willing to take hold of a lowly mind and act through it upon the world. If He has anything to say to His wandering and benighted children, He is sure to speak through the man who is transcendently humble. Good and evil are so intense, pervasive, unrestingly competitive, that where one is not the other must be. God wants to speak to the world; for if He is indeed its Father, His heart is charged with infinite thoughts and solicitudes, and when He waits long and speaks not, it is because He cannot find the meek and single-minded messenger. Wherever a heart is lowly enough to be the channel of His Word, He cannot be silent, and the fulness of the message is proportioned in every case to the meekness and self-renunciation of the herald. The Word would lose its Divine distinctiveness if it came through one set upon bringing about his own honour. A self-exalting man must ever speak out of a dull, dim, uninspired, God-deserted soul. Or, to change the metaphor to one used by our Lord Himself, wherever there is the single eye the spring of overflowing light will be near by. Jesus was more absolutely God's herald than others, the giver of a more wonderful revelation to those who were waiting at His feet, because His humility was supreme.

Absolute humility implies not only fitness to become God's messenger, but a foregoing intimacy and contact with God which qualifies its possessor to interpret His nature and counsels. The pompous, self-exalting person is generally one who has lived much with inferiors. When we meet with pre-eminent modesty, we find, as a rule, that it is a tribute to minds of outstanding force, strength, clearness, with which there has been past converse. That detachment from self and a vainglorious world we see in Jesus Christ, can only arise through a pre-existing attachment to one who is characterised by boundless spiritual power and fascination. If we see a man content to forego his own interest and reputation in furthering some cause which is laid upon his heart, closing his eyes to the promise and prospect of earthly honour and power, submitting to ignominy without a murmur, yea, courting death itself in his enterprise for another's glory, we are quite sure that his affections have been stirred by the direct personal knowledge of Him in whose name the life-work is pushed to its last heroic conclusions. It is not for some mythical hero he does all this, not for some dreamy demi-god who looms through the haze of antiquity, not for one about whom he has dreamed in a mood of frenzied imagination, but for a being he has directly known, and learned to love with a passion which quenches self. The surpassing humility of Jesus is a token that He is responding to a presence veiled from those who are less lowly. He is marked out by this unmistakable trait as an authentic witness of the Divine character, and a duly accredited messenger of the Divine command.

Did the Teacher, so far as we may claim to know Him through the historical record, answer to His own test? Is He vindicated by the ethical canon to which He appeals?

To point out all the illustrations of His strange humility would be to tell the story of His life afresh from its beginning to its close. This significant grace was the key to His many years of repression whilst toiling as a common workman at Nazareth. His baptism and its attendant incidents were blazoned with this wonderful sign. He took His stand side by side with open sinners as though He were one of themselves, and accepted this rite of the great evangelical reform at the hands of a man who, because of his limitation of religious privilege, filled a lowlier place than the meanest disciple of the New Covenant. How unwilling we are to accept anything from those who may seem to be less worthy or less gifted than ourselves! It seems suicidal to legitimate reputation. To meet the pride of human life, it is assumed the Church must have its princes, who shall be the social equals of the highest of those to whom they minister. From one who wore the rough dress of a hunter and declared himself unworthy to be this Great Teacher's slave, He besought the favour of baptism. His chosen methods of work discredited Him with the classes who held the reins of power, and whose approval would have had the highest possible value to Him if He had been of this world. Whilst we see in Him no trace of the blustering reformer, no bias towards cynicism or hot-tempered declamation, none of the weak versatility of the man who, having forfeited popularity with one stratum of society, seeks to recover it by championing another, He was never careful to conciliate. When unsought honour was thrust upon Him, for once in His life He turned His back and fled. And how meekly He bowed Himself to the ignominy of a death against which the base-born slave might justly rebel! If egotism is latent in any part of a man's nature, there is nothing like undeserved suffering to bring it out. This Saint of saints accepts a felon's death without once contrasting it with His own high deserts. Was it no triumph of humility to silently surrender Himself to the death and reproach of the cross? Did He who chose the gibbet rather than an earthly throne; insult, spitting, profane opprobrium, rather than the cheers of the grateful multitude,—seek His own glory, or that of Him from whose presence He had come?

The conditions under which this humility was displayed only served to emphasise its surprising depth and its complete sincerity. From His birth Mary had honoured Him as never babe was honoured before, and unconsciously led Him to expect deference from others. In the household at Nazareth it was understood that He was a crown-prince, and at the most plastic period of His life He was encircled with homage which seemed to perpetuate the romantic adoration at His cradle. The poor dullard, the whipped serf, the destined laggard in the race of life, is humble in some superficial fashion, because pretence would make him the butt of common laughter. He who is born to menial work, with no spark of wit in his brain, fated to displease his fellows by saying the wrong thing and acting in the wrong way, sometimes resigns himself to his pitiful destiny, and slouches through life without assuming that he has had the right to anybody's favour or praise. But if we look at Jesus Christ from the lower intellectual standpoint only, there was genius in His veins. He could not be blind to His own power of winning men; and if to any one the temptation could come to ask a large share of popularity, as mere justice it must have come to our Lord. The humility of One who has scarcely reached the prime of life must always be notable and rare. Youth is full of hope, energy, ambition, restless project, and has yet to learn its limitations. After long, sharp, weary lessons, men become humble at last. When they have been often disappointed, made to see again and again how tiny is their power of controlling human affairs, and how egregiously they overestimated themselves when setting out upon the race of life, they acquire in the end a chastened spirit, which is akin to humility. It is rare to find a youth who has learned the lesson, and rarer still to find one who has anticipated it. Yet from the cradle to the workshop, and from the workshop to the baptismal flood, and from the baptismal flood to the cross, Jesus was free from vain egotism and all feverish desire for His own honour and distinction. Is not such humility incomparable? If God be about to speak to men, is not such an one marked out as His Messenger. At the outset Jesus requires only the acknowledgment of His authority as a God-sent Teacher. From that initial admission we must surely and swiftly pass to higher levels of faith.

CHAPTER IV.

THE MORAL PREPARATION FOR FAITH.

RELIGIOUS unbelief is often dealt with by two extreme and mistaken methods: by that of a narrow and angry Philistinism on the one hand, and by that of a loose and dulcet sentimentality on the other. There are those amongst us who assume that a man who does not believe in God, or in the revelation of God through Jesus Christ, is a moral monstrosity. They are prepared to believe anything bad about his disposition or private conduct, and are quite sure his state of mind must be connected with unwholesome aberrations. They study him with the same creepy and morbid interest as Lambroso might feel when studying a striking case in criminology. Such prejudiced assumptions are ignorant, unjust, and mischievous in the last degree. Whilst there are terrible moral perils in atheism against which the warning voice must be ever lifted, the character of the atheist is not always determined by his unhappy theory. Slander, when even vague and promiscuous, will do the devil's work and strengthen the side of unbelief. But over against this angry Philistinism there is a soft, easy-going, unctuous sentimentality, with a shrewd eye for the line of least resistance, which works as much mischief in the opposite direction. It treats unbelief as though no moral question however subtle lay behind it,—as an intellectual misfortune over which the man himself has no more control than the possessor of a wry neck, a crooked leg, a freckled and bewarted face, has over his physical defect. He was born with a bias towards doubt. He has an innate crazé for taking sides with the opposition. His education, his surroundings, his prescribed courses of study, have made his negations inevitable. Character has no more bearing upon the man's mental condition than upon a sum in arithmetic, for in nine cases out of ten the man who traverses the same ground will find himself in the same agnostic mood. And thus it comes to pass that the treatment received by unbelief in its many sad and persistent phases, like the treatment of some ill-starred child, oscillates between the unreasoning cuff and the equally unreasoning caress.

It is no such one-sided view that our Lord takes when He expostulates with the Jews for their unbelief. Whilst refraining from malicious and exaggerated charges, He yet recognises with robust fidelity that the disqualification for faith is often moral. "How can ye believe which receive honour one of another, and seek not the honour that cometh from God only?" Undue sensitiveness to the opinions of others may form the gravest possible impediment to confidence in God and His messengers. Pride always unfits for complete faith in God and submission to His holy mandate. Unbelief, though not always identified with lawlessness of act, is often the product of a secret and blameworthy temper of soul. A commanding passion for the praise of men may shut its subject out from all faith in God and His redemptive agencies. The lack of faith, if traced back to its deepest causes, is thus invested with a moral significance and made amenable to the judgement of God.

Our unbelief will be a foregone conclusion if that section of popular opinion with which we want to keep in accord is hostile to spiritual faith, as it was in the time of Christ. For many diverse and complex reasons the feeling of the leaders of Jewish thought was hostile to the Galilean movement. If a vote had been snatched in the great ecclesiastical council, when Joseph, Nicodemus, and Gamaliel happened to be absent, the condemnation of this Carpenter-Prophet and His claims would probably have been carried without a dissentient voice. Of course they all believed in the Jehovah of tradition, but not in a living Jehovah who would act in unexpected ways, and send a Messenger with claims ludicrously disproportionate to the obscurity of His birth and His surroundings. And that permanent committee of all the talents in Jerusalem wielded a power perhaps greater than that of the press in modern times. It minted public opinion, and put upon it the inscription it was thought expedient for it to bear. He who held himself bound to follow the leading of this powerful hierarchy could no more come to faith in Jesus Christ, than any one of a dozen barges towed in the wake of a steam tug can take its own independent channel. Whilst a man made the applause of his contemporaries the supreme wish of his life, he could only get into those tracks of opinion and judgement whither it was the will of the supreme council to lead.

Jewish history ought to have been admonitory. It showed how Ahab could cajole a school of four hundred prophets, with Zedekiah at their head, into a prophecy that was beautifully unanimous, and at the same time fatally misleading. It told the story of a prophet of God who brought death upon himself by giving heed to the pleasant flattery of a brother prophet, rather than to the Divine voice that spoke directly to his own conscience. And yet official coteries of spurious piety carried on an enormous business in the manufacture of public opinion still. Faith in the new evangel was impossible within the circle of such influence. He who was eager for the smile of official favour could not believe.

And it is perhaps equally difficult to believe when faith is fashionable and men are moved by the desire to stand well with the community. A make-believe faith is apt to thrust itself forward to answer the demands of society, just as every possible specimen of Birmingham coloured glass is thrust upon the traveller the moment he lands in a country famous for its precious stones. But may not public opinion turn round and encourage faith? and in that case will not the man who is most sensitive to the praise or blame of his fellows have an advantage over the man who is indifferent to the judgements of his contemporaries? May there not be golden ages in which it is held to be a proper and necessary thing that men should believe? and under such conditions will not the man have an advantage in the cultivation of faith who is quick to feel the judgement of his contemporaries? As a matter of fact, do not some possess faith who have a marked weakness for human applause, and who perhaps never would have possessed it had not the prestige of the leaders in the State and in society been used on Christ's side? Without depreciating the value of human authority in conducting men to the threshold of faith, or challenging the expediency of the attempt to invest religion with as much of social influence as can be engaged upon its side without corrupt compromise, the fact must still be recognised that faith is a spiritual creation of the living God Himself, and He will never come to operate in hearts where the honour coming from man is preferred to that of which He is the supreme fountain. Faith cannot wake up to life within us till the love of God's approbation is paramount.

This preference of human to Divine approval qualifies the confession a man may make of the supremacy of God. It assumes that the contribution to his well-being made by a fellow-creature is more significant and commanding than that made by the great Creator Himself. It accounts man's favour and commendation of transcendent value, and puts him, poor erring mortal that he is, in the most commanding place, whilst it relegates God, who has become little more than an abstract theory, to the background of life. In the heart which thus idolises a fellow-mortal and clings to his favour there is veiled atheism, which is of course the negation of faith both in God and in God's Son. The principle underlying our Lord's remonstrance with the Jews is, that a man is unable to believe whilst he is wedded to practical unbelief and cherishes tempers which are its unmistakable symptoms. The Divine praise is not quite so real or so soul-satisfying as that of man whose breath is in his nostrils. If a native of India should declare his belief in the stability of the Indian Government and of the banks established under its charter, and should at the same time put all his wealth into portable jewellery or hoard it in the mud-walls of his perishable house, he would belie by his act all lip-tributes of confidence. The pathetic pertinacity with which a man clings to his neighbour's approbation is the sign of a lost faith in God. God's praise, if He condescend to praise, must be more than man's, inasmuch as He rules and shapes destiny and is the source of all power and authority. It means victories, crowns, sceptres, dominions. He who courts the flatteries of his weak and short-lived fellows shows that he has no faith in the worth or reality of God's praise. This love of applause is the sign of a changed trust, the mark of a half-suppressed idolatry of soul. The millionaire whose nerves have been unstrung by earthquake, and who is living like a common gipsy in a tent on the seashore, and refusing to go back to the carpets and pictures and silver of his villa on the hillside, shows that the confidence he once had in the strength and stability of his own elegant home has been shaken. Whilst a man honours his fellow above God by preferring his smile and approbation, he must necessarily account the witness of man greater than that of God, and cannot receive God's testimony concerning His Son. A humility which renounces the world, despising alike its smiles and its frowns, is the first condition of faith.

The subtle processes by which faith is awakened and developed are neutralised by the desire for earthly honour and reputation. The faith inculcated by our Lord has its rootfibres in secret spiritual motives and affections. It arises through direct manifestations of God's character and purpose to the soul, of a most refined and delicate quality. The mind out of sympathy with God is incapable of discerning intimacy with the Divine nature, and government, and aim; and without that no strong and solid principle of belief can exist. An unrestrained love of human applause is always associated with this lack of a sympathetic attitude towards God and His inward communications. A man covets most the praise of those he is inclined to love best. If a desire for the honour God bestows is not our controlling passion, we must ever be unresponsive to those influences which emanate from His presence to quicken faith in the children of men. Some time ago an English naturalist described the method he used to test the power of scent in a dog which had accompanied him for six or seven years in his shooting expeditions. Having shut up the dog in a room of the house in which he was staying, he asked a number of gillies and fellow-sportsmen to follow in his footsteps as he led them for a walk through the fields. After going for some distance the file broke up into two, he leading one party in one direction and the others going off at right angles. The dog was then let loose. It caught up its master's trail and followed him, although a dozen other feet had been planted in his steps. When it reached the point at which the party divided it was puzzled for a moment, but at last followed the procession led by its master. A dog fed and fondled by a dozen different hands could not have stood a test of that character. It was led along the right track by its attachment to its owner. The world is full of intercrossing leadings, natural and spiritual influences blending with each along all our pathways of movement. He who is unduly sensitive to the world's praise and blame cannot follow the path of a God-directed faith. He will be dull and insensible to the highest and the holiest leadings. Resolute single-mindedness is the foregoing condition of all true belief in God and God's Redeeming Son. He whose heart is charged with pride and ambition will find himself as perplexed as the man who is listening at the telephone in a thunderstorm, when the insulation of the wires is momentarily impaired, and confusing fragments of many messages are heard.

In declaring that self-seeking pride was a disqualification for faith, our Lord had doubtless in view that mystery of His own humiliation which was by and by to become the great subject-matter of faith. That the Son had come forth from the Father to a lot of obloquy, reproach, and pain, must ever be incredible to those whose lives are ruled by worldly ambition. That He did not seek His own glory He had already declared was the sign that He had come forth from God; but the sign could only appeal to those in whom meek and lowly tempers were already dawning. It is hard to believe in that, some faint earnest of which we do not find in our own souls. A man cannot believe facts which are in the very teeth of his instinctive affinities and dispositions. The head-hunters of Borneo would necessarily treat as fables the thousand and one humane institutions which are the products of Christian civilisation. A race of colour-blind barbarians, if such a race existed, would ridicule the idea of finding out the elements of which distant stars are fashioned by observing the bands and lines of colour disclosed by the spectroscope. There must be the beginning of vision in us if we are to receive the fairy tales of the microscopist and the astronomer. God can be made known to us only in those aspects in which we desire, however faintly, to be like Him. To the heart which craves pomp and worldly applause with intense desire and unvarying consistency, it must ever be a hopeless paradox that one in the form of God should empty Himself. That the Divine Son should have entered into shame and reproach and curse for others, must be a hard saying to the man who hungers for the homage of his fellows. The Jews could not understand one who did not seek glory from His fellow-countrymen. Pride made this wonderful mission of love and humiliation an enigma.

The belief our Lord sought was to be full of tender, evangelical trustfulness, and the desire for human praise was an effectual bar to that. By the exaggerated and undeserved esteem of others, men are built up in habits of proud defiance. They cannot realise that one who makes for himself a great reputation amongst his fellows does not stand equally well with God, and must needs be forgiven and saved by sacrificial processes. By the flattering verdict of friends and contemporaries, a man's will is stiffened against God's verdict upon his state and standing. Those deep moral dissatisfactions, which are the birth-pangs of contrite and saving faith, are countervailed. No wonder that the praying publican became capable and conscious of a soul-comforting faith, whilst the Pharisee retired unblessed; for it was useless for the one to seek human commendation, but the other steeped therein every power and sensibility of his life.

In tracing back unbelief to pride by this trenchant interrogatory, our Lord implied that faith took its rise in moral conditions, and that men were responsible for the measure of it they attained. The Jews blamed our Lord for their hesitation and unbelief, implying that it was inevitable because of the ambiguity of His declarations. Our Lord put back responsibility for unbelief upon His hearers. "How can ye believe which receive honour one of another, and seek not the honour which cometh from God only?" The single eye sees Divine realities. The mystery is revealed to babes; saving wisdom is learned by the meek and lowly in heart. Whilst our Lord asserts again and again His Father's sovereignty, He implies with equal frequency that man's free agency has its place in questions of faith as well as in questions of conduct.

CHAPTER V.

HUMAN FREEDOM AND DIVINE POWER.

WHILST our Lord firmly asserts that the hindrances to faith are moral, and will disappear from the path of the man who seeks to put himself into a right relation with God, He at the same time upholds the sovereignty of Divine power in the process of salvation, and declares that there can be no limit to the ranges of that power. The retreating figure of the rich young ruler, who had only one step more to take into the kingdom, was yet in view,—an object-lesson of the fatal spell of gold, as Jesus exclaims, " It is easier for a camel to go through the eye of a needle." The disciples, amazed and half stupefied at the severity of the Master's tone, are brought back to hope and to heart by His avowal that " the things which are impossible with men are possible with God." In Matthew's and Mark's account of the incident the statement is yet stronger. Not only does God's power transcend all human forthputtings of moral energy, but in the realm of mind it is just as infinite and absolute as in the realm of matter. "All things are possible with God." Grace is omnipotent, and invests in mysterious ways the realm of man's moral freedom.

The rich young ruler went away from the Great Teacher's presence, saying, as all men who find difficulties in their path are prone to say, "I cannot," which, put into blunt, candid, less euphonious phrase, meant "I will not." So men ever disguise with refined hypocrisies their evil wilfulness. "I cannot" and "I will not" are by no means synonymous terms, as the necessarian so often assumes.

It is of the power which tells in the spiritual world that our Lord speaks, and that is of an entirely different order and quality from the power whose manifestations excite our reverent wonder in the system of nature. Moral influence is distinct from that life-creating and life-sustaining and life-moulding force which operates through the spaces of the visible universe. Omnipotence is commonly classified by the theologians as one of God's natural attributes, but it has its counterpart in the higher side of the Divine personality. The ever-active forces of God's truth, righteousness, love, are incalculable in their sum,—and moral is a sublimer thing than natural omnipotence, counting for more in the final well-being of the universe. It expresses a deeper and a more subtle essence in the life of the Godhead.

There is a force which fashions suns, and impels the movements producing their huge stores of heat,—a force which sustains the march of constellations through terms of time that mock our little earthly history, a force which drives the tides and sweeps through the tempests, a force which vivifies and upholds the restless and ever-extending mystery of life, a force which rules the rise and the fall of empires and civilisations, and that force is infinite. But from the same spring there issues a less obtrusive force belonging to another order of operations,—the force which detaches man from his idols; the force which frees him from the legion evils that have trampled his greatness in the dust, which makes sympathies and antipathies strangely change places in his nature, so that he comes to hate what he loved and to love what he once hated; the force which works out the new creations of the gospel,—and that force is no less infinite though it is dealing with persons rather than things. In the realm of thought, morals, human conduct, God's power is just as far-reaching as in the realm of physics. It is true, He has clothed man with moral attributes He does not see fit to disparage or disregard, but He has clothed cosmic atoms with other attributes also which His immanent power in nature also respects. This was a comparatively rare thought to the Jews. They had been so accustomed to look for God's power in outward things, that they were almost oblivious of the forces which act upon human character and effect its noblest transformations.

That Almighty God cannot force a human will, making a man act counter to his own choice, is a theological axiom with us. He will never put upon man a pressure which will suspend or efface the power of self-determination. It is a part of His original decree not to do it, and He cannot have constituted man free so that this prerogative may be abrogated. He has marked out certain tracts of human thought and action into which He will never come as a resistless dictator. But at the same time God's power over human hearts can never be measured by man's. His power surpasses all human possibilities, and when He has given due and plenary acknowledgment to the moral freedom of man, He can still do that which is beyond the utmost range of human strength to accomplish. In the moral no less than in the physical universe, Jesus would have His Father's infinite sovereignty amply recognised.

The mechanical analogies used in describing the mysterious function of the human will are ambiguous and misleading, and we speak of the necessity which compels it to follow the strongest motives without rightly apprehending the part the will itself plays in creating those motives and adjusting their weight. We too often conceive of it as a pair of scales dipping this way or that, as it is plied with temptations to evil on the one hand or incitements to good on the other. Such illustrations make the principle of self-determination in human nature entirely passive, and allow it no place whatever in the transactions of the daily life.

If mechanical illustrations can help our comprehension of the question at all, it is perhaps as well to fall back upon the primitive device with which the Eastern peasant draws water from well, cistern, or canal to irrigate his field. Attached to an upright piece of wood there is a free-moving crossbeam, to one end of which a stone is bound, whilst a bucket hangs from the other. The balance between the two is so nearly equal, that by a slight expenditure of strength the peasant can lower his bucket into the well, and with the help of the counterpoising stone can bring back the brimming bucket to the surface. In an operation of that sort the man counts for something, and if the work of irrigation stops it is not so much because bucket outweighs stone or stone bucket, but because the peasant himself has gone to sleep. On both the good and evil sides of man's life motives of vast weight are brought to bear, but his will occupies the midway position between the two, and determines conduct and destiny. And more than that, the will has power to bring into use or set aside the immeasurable stores of motive which lie around it. As a matter of fact, motives are always changing their force and their preponderance in the scheme of our lives, and we ourselves are the magicians and perform marvels of transformation. We do this, it is true, in virtue of other forces which lie outside us awaiting our use, rather than through the inherent qualities of our own personality and life. Whilst, however, we recognise the province of human choice, we must not forget to pay our homage to those special forms of influence which co-operate with the will and act upon it, directing, shaping, and invigorating without robbing it of its original attributes.

How far may the Divine power assert itself over man's thought and character without dethroning his will?

Divine power may at least outmatch the power of evil in man's environment without running the slightest risk of annulling his moral responsibility. It is bound to do that at the very least, if the will is to be kept free to assert itself on the side of right. The passions of the flesh convert themselves into motives which are a continuous incitement to evil. They make the great crimes and tragedies of human history, often measuring themselves defiantly against all the resources of law and civilisation. And these passions act with that cumulative, social force described under the New Testament term "world," inclining groups, communities, whole races, to what is base, sordid, brutish. And over and above these normal passions man is plied with mysterious and persistent solicitations to selfishness, wrong-doing, unspiritual views which take their rise in the realms of the unseen. The whole constitution of human society at times seems as though it were under the direct rule and authority of the devil himself, and as though the devil were something bigger even than a fallen archangel. The evil that is in the world is despotic, sweeping, tremendous, but it does not bring about the universal annihilation of man's will-power; for God's power in secret and subtle ways overpasses the utmost power of evil that works in the world, and keeps man's moral freedom unimpaired under the most threatening conditions. The force that operates to save men must at least be coequal and co-extensive with the unknown energies and operations of evil. The things which are impossible to either men or devils must be possible to God in the kingdom of grace, or men might plead that they were shut up in conditions of moral neutrality by forces acting upon them from opposite sides, and just counterpoising each other. It is something for us to recognise the fact that the Divine power which enables for good exceeds both the natural and supernatural forces which tend to draw aside to evil. It is to be feared that men's homage to the Divine sovereignty in the kingdom of grace does not always rise to that imperfect level even. God's power must assert itself against all those powers of evil which operate in human nature to keep it in selfishness and transgression.

The Divine power transcends the energies inherent in the human will; and of the range of those energies, both for good and for evil, we have a very inadequate conception. This moral faculty seems to have been endowed with all but boundless potencies, and it can be the subject of gigantic constraints without losing the power of reasserting itself. In bestowing this gift upon man, God seems to have stopped little short of making His creature equal with Himself. Volition is an attribute of Titanic proportions, and it is alone amongst the other parts of man's nature in its transcendent greatness. The force of the will for evil baffles imagination to realise. The ingenuities of cruelty cannot vanquish it, generations of oppression cannot outweary or exterminate it, the combined forces of civilisation cannot enslave it. God may find here a sphere in which He may perhaps show forth more of the plenitude of that power to which nothing is impossible than in any other part of His universe.

But it may be said that thus far, whilst God has the human will to reckon with and is bound to recognise its original prerogatives, His power, though vast, is not demonstrably infinite, and Matthew's version of our Lord's words, " With God all things are possible," is scarcely justified. To that it must be answered, those last reserves of power which bear the marks of God's absolute infinitude, and attest Him just as almighty in the realm of mind as in the realm of matter, are vouchsafed, not merely where there is the passive consent, but the active solicitation of the human will. Our Lord introduces the necessary qualification in His address to the father of the tormented youth at the foot of the Mount of Transfiguration. "If thou canst believe, all things are possible to him that believeth." Whilst God will bring the unconditional power of His sovereignty to bear in counteracting the forces which weaken and deprave human life so as to keep man in a state of freedom and moral accountability, we are not bound to think that He will assert His almightiness in natures deliberately shut against the power of His grace. Where the will resists, God may operate upon it with incommensurable forces, for it is sometimes phenomenal in its antagonism to God and goodness; but where the will consents, God puts forth the same plenitude of strength which dwelt in the coequal Son, and so to their last jot and tittle the words are vindicated, "With God all things are possible."

We may estimate this power in part by observing those forces of discipline which are everywhere present in human life. Whatever enigmas may baffle our interpretation for the time being in the subrational kingdoms of nature, we can scarcely be blind to the fact that all the forces which environ human society are welded into instruments and vehicles of moral and spiritual discipline. The ground on which we pitch our tents trembles and quivers still in vague sympathy with the solemnity and significance of Divine law. God teaches men the vanity of resisting His will, and sooner or later the illusiveness of every form of transgression and folly. In many ways He "chastises man for his offences, and makes his beauty to consume away like the moth." The order of nature is moulded to moral uses. Man has little need to devise for himself penances and self-mortifications, for providence has them ready for all, and the royal rebel is brought low by the stripes, pains, and burdens which are laid again and again upon the body. The most infatuated are often broken in at last by His strong and heavy hand. A man whom the Saviour loved and who would not make the complete surrender, might well go away sorrowful, for he was setting his face towards scorching ordeals of tribulation rather than to ease, luxury, and physical well-being. The power which works impossibilities is spiritual in its essential qualities, but it asserts itself through God's providential administration of common things. God's disciplines are sharper, more complex, more ingeniously and effectually combined, than we know, and bring to pass that which is inconceivable to man. He counteracts the spell of riches. For the one wedded to his great possessions He provides unknown and often bitter methods of disillusionment. The man whose charities have to be drawn out of him by a process more violent than the dentistry applied to the mediæval Jews, grows lavish and finds in sacrifice an undreamt-of paradise. The millionaire and the saint meet in the same man, and greater things come to pass than the miracle of a burdened, hulking, ungainly camel threading its way through the needle's eye.

The power which achieves the things impossible to men is commensurate with the infinite excellencies of the Divine character. The range and intensity of the moral influence going forth from one member of human society to play upon another, are determined by the proportions of the character from which it emanates, and by the degree of inspiration that character is capable of receiving from the character and personality of others. The whole weight of the Divine character is brought to bear upon those who are rendered plastic to its impressions by the disciplines of the present life. The power of God in the spiritual universe and over spiritual beings is boundless, for it is the ever-active immanence of His essential holiness. He can make men feel those immeasurable forces of moral energy which create worlds of pure and unselfish activity, and sustain through uncounted generations a more perfect life than any of which we dream. He can make men feel the strength of those moral energies which were pulsating in the Son from before all time, and putting upon Him the stamp of supreme spiritual worth. In declaring God's moral almightiness, Jesus realised that through Himself that indomitable life of truth and charity which had been His eternal possession was to be communicated to a renewed world. It was His work to make men sensible of what was deepest, most sacred, most active in God, and so to invigorate men with motives of transcendent power. In that new kingdom established amongst men we are not shut up to human possibilities only. God's power over the human heart and life outsoars ours as the vastness of His truth, righteousness, fidelity, love, surpass all finite spiritual excellencies. When He touches men in Christ Jesus with the forces of His own living and wonderful character, impossibility becomes an obsolete word, and all things grow within range of attainment. .

The power which consummates that which was once impossible is indicated by the range of the new truths brought to light for man's salvation.

The two salient truths which slowly unveil themselves in our Lord's life and death, the incarnation and the atonement, may be looked upon as the scale of this power. The heathen world was familiar enough with degenerate forms of these two ideas, but heathen fictions of incarnation and sacrifice were wedded to fatalistic philosophies of the origin of things, and did not represent voluntary acts of humiliation and self-devoting love. From the standpoint of human selfishness the facts of which the manger and the cross afterwards became symbols were unthinkable. These doctrines, when developed, were not to be mere speculations competing for ascendancy with speculations a little less noble and a little less inspiring, but were forms of truth to be filled to their uttermost dimensions with the living power of God Most High. Sometimes these dogmas are empty letters only, and men utter them without feeling the spell of their power. One does not wonder at the revolt of the intellect and the conscience when they are theological shibboleths and nothing more. These doctrines are forms through which the greatness of the Divine power is to work, bodies into which the breath that vitalises the universe is to come, and what wonders they would achieve if we found them always vibrant with Divine influence! We may measure God's possibilities through these conceptions, which, till our hearts are touched from on high, paralyse us also with wondering incredulity. Such truths, divinely vitalised, must surely work that which man judges to be beyond the horizon of practical life or sober expectation. These vast thoughts give us some standard by which to estimate the degree of His influence over the human mind and character. The immensity of love demonstrated in the facts of redemption brings new quickening to the conscience, new fire to the affections, new control to the will. Under such views of things, the rich young ruler may at last have felt the justice of what at the outset seemed an extravagant and irrational demand, and have made haste to lay his all at the pierced feet of Jesus Christ. The impossible assumes new aspects in the light of these revelations, and becomes one of the common possibilities in the kingdom of God.

Again and again our Lord recognised these human impossibilities which appalled the disciples, and not only soberly reckoned with them, but revelled in the sense of victory over them. "Except a man be born again." Impossible and absurd! thought Nicodemus. "Except ye eat my flesh, and drink my blood, ye have no life in you," and "No man can come to me except the Father draw him." Revolting and unthinkable doctrine! How could the God of all majesty so invert the reason of things, as to clothe with soul-renewing and life-conveying virtue and fascination the bloody spectacle of the gibbet, and so win men to faith and worship? "Ye believe not, because ye are not my sheep." If to believe is one and the same thing with transmigration into a new species, how can that be brought to pass? What must be said to the man with a congenital incapacity for religion, or what is perhaps more appalling still, for morals? These statements and similitudes emphasise the fact that most of the things required by our Lord were impossible to men. And unless it had been so there would have been no call for that new revelation of grace and power He had set Himself to make. He had come to achieve what was utterly impracticable from the human standpoint, and wished to accentuate the fact again and again. "What is thy name?" "Legion, for we are many." The trampling hosts of evil had swept through the poor victim's soul, destroying the glory of its early promise, like a mad and frenzied army raging through fields of ripening corn. A poor, bowed, wasting, defenceless weakling against six thousand armed Romans. The sequel serves to show that the things impossible to men are possible to God.

If we look upon the worst habits as incurable, the most flagrant offenders as irredeemable, vice as a factor to be catered for by nominally Christian governments to the end of human history, the man most hopelessly bound to his idols as incapable of learning to love God with all his soul and mind and strength, we dishonour that sovereign power in the realm of mind which our Lord came to proclaim and illustrate and apply.

CHAPTER VI.

THE RACIAL LIMITATIONS OF THE MINISTRY.

"I AM not sent but to the lost sheep of the house of Israel," was the Master's stern and apparently ungracious reply to the melting appeal of a Syro-Phœnician mother for her afflicted child. This declaration must not be looked upon as a piece of grim pleasantry with which the Great Teacher tested an importunate woman's faith. It embodies an important fact at the root of which many principles lie; for in the words of the commission addressed to the apostles He lays down the same limitation. They must follow in His own footsteps, and for the term of His personal ministry amongst them seek first for the lost sheep of the house of Israel. The Son of man came to seek and to save Zaccheus, "forasmuch as he also was a son of Abraham."

In our Lord's humanity there had been implanted the germinal instinct of a double relationship,—a special relationship to the Jews, and a more comprehensive relationship, not only to the Jews, but to the entire Gentile world, whose sin he was sent to expiate by His sacrifice of love. We may perhaps compare that humanity to the stock into which two different kinds of buds have been engrafted, timed to open in an earlier and a later month. Deep-folded within His thought there was the sense of this saving work He was to achieve on behalf of every man without distinction of race. But before that catholic culmination could be reached, there was a divinely implanted sense of obligation to the Jews as their heaven-sent Teacher and King which must be fulfilled; and the later and broader idea could not be suffered to thwart by its premature germination and efflorescence the earlier and more restricted part of His vocation. Like Peter, His first apostle, He Himself must be "a minister to the circumcision."

And in this introductory part of His task He must not wantonly clash with Jewish insularity, and exasperate a prejudice that might seem to be more or less ignoble. It was no mere outcry of clannish pride which in the beginning bade the Israelites withdraw themselves from the heathen. By habits of rigid separation only could they preserve the tender virtue and quality of their providential training and inheritance, and to sequester them from the world was the quarantine heaven prescribed to guard them against the contaminations of superstition and idolatry. Their exclusiveness had come to associate itself with evil and degenerate tempers and conceits, but Jesus will not needlessly affront prejudices which were once lofty principles. If He place Himself athwart habits and customs which in their beginnings were the rules of religious self-preservation, He cannot deliver His message to the satisfaction of His own conscience, and make known that passion of long-suffering and pitying tenderness which He has in common with the Father. For the full term of His ministry He must concentrate His personal thought and labour upon the Jews, so that the last hours of their day of grace may not be cut short, and in the time of judgement the long-suffering love of God may be found to have left them without excuse.

As a spectacle of corporate backsliding, the nation has a peculiar claim upon the compassion of its King, and indulgence must be exercised towards all hereditary customs which are not obviously sins. This favoured race, with a mere handful of exceptions, was wofully astray from God, but the saved remnant of it was to become the seed of that Church Jesus came to set up amongst men. A nation that had stood so high, and was trembling to so deep a fall, our Lord justly felt must have the first claim upon His ministry. The backslider, be he the individual man or that aggregate of men we call a race, has stood nearer than others to the heart of God, and, alas! sinks through rebellion into a more appalling doom. The tragedy of sin reaches its crowning agony in the headlong plunge into ruin of one who had once escaped its toils and for a time had been brought nigh unto God. So at least thought this pitiful and sympathetic man, Jesus of Nazareth; for though He was awake to the spectacle of human wretchedness, and His tense insight haunted Him till His visage seemed to become one with that of the sufferer himself, He was so absorbed by His thoughts of the woebegone, peril-hunted, doom-awaiting wanderers of the house of Israel, that He had no ears for the cry of a Gentile woman, and treated her at the outset with as much indifference as the most phlegmatic of us. The paramount desire of the moment which seemed to possess Him and make Him forgetful of strangers and aliens, was deep solicitude for those who epitomised in their passing history the guilt of apostasy and the terrors of its fast-approaching destruction.

Can we see beneath these forbidding words, and discern reasons for the limitations in the range of our Lord's personal ministry?

Four or five things may be said in justification of the policy adopted by the Great Teacher.

In husbanding His resources for an appeal to a prepared people, Jesus made the best possible use of the few short months of His active ministry. It was no long life of public service that lay before Him. He whose term of teaching upon earth is but a handbreadth, must needs focus and concentrate His efforts upon those who may be justly expected to respond to them.

He aimed at utilising pre-existing ideas in His task of enlightening and saving men. He was conservative of all the undeveloped good that was still sleeping in human hearts, and counted the holy memories of the past amongst His most effectual allies.

By seeking first the lost sheep of the house of Israel, Jesus put honour upon the work of the preceding ages, and vindicated His place as a consummator of the kings and prophets and righteous men of olden time. He did not despise the toil of a single predecessor in the service of His Father, however lowly, and felt that toil must surely bear some fruit in His own generation. Unlike many who bear His name, He did not set Himself to minimise what had been achieved in bygone days, and assume that no single step had been gained towards the reconstruction of society. The earlier messengers of the Most High had done something for the Jewish mind, and He was jealous for their work.

This rigidly defined mission to the lost sheep of the house of Israel was a sign of His faith in the fact that throughout the past ages the Spirit of the Father had been at work in the world, and especially upon the race to which He belonged, and preparing it for His own last ministry of redemption. He could not turn aside from the Jew as though He Himself had no faith in the Old Testament histories and their record of God's past visitations of His people. He must honour the providential preparation of the earlier epochs.

He best served the Gentiles by leaving them out of His reckoning for the time. He wished to teach their teachers, and His words would have been lost to the after-generations unless He had spoken to a people schooled by the history of centuries to understand them. In the end the Gentiles gained by what seemed at the outset a harsh and narrow policy, and the paradox stands revealed as a truism, that Christ makes His mission world-wide by limiting the range of His personal action.

Jesus felt that He had been sent to use and build up as far as might be the work already existing in human souls. He was not callous to the needs of this woman, nor blind to the faith of a Roman centurion, nor unsympathetic to the Greeks who on one of His last visits to the Temple desired to see Him. It was to vindicate the rights and privileges of the Gentiles that He drove out the traders from His Father's house, and first drew upon His head the hatred of the priests. In the closing twilight that fell upon His brief life He thinks of "the sheep who are of other folds." Those who are afar off must in due time be visited and be brought nigh, and the evangel which has its centre at Jerusalem, and its first circle in Samaria, must reach in ever-expanding enterprises of love to the uttermost parts of the earth. But He did not go to the Gentiles at once, although He might possibly have found for Himself a more kindly welcome than amongst the Jews.

A traveller in the forests of Guiana tells us that it is possible to trace the footsteps of man where nature has reconquered for herself both the camping ground of the Indian, and the plantation of the Dutch settler two or three centuries later. The citron, the bread-fruit, the pine-apple, the cassava, the capsicum, never thrive where man has not first planted them, and degenerate types of these plants in the thick tangle of the forest show that man has once been there. He who proposes to clear and resettle the forest, and dreams that he will develop the plants he needs for the purpose of his life from the weeds of the forest and the thickets of the jungle, rather than foster anew the plants which have been improved by human skill for thousands of years, would prove himself a fool by the very project. In a nation overspread by the rank growths of greed, unbelief, and practical heathenism, the skilled eye of the Lord could discern the ancient roots and upspringings of holier things, and He would not have been shrewd and discerning and statesman-like if He had passed by the Jew and his wonderful history. Underneath the bigotry, arrogance, and formalism of the ruling classes, there were the rudiments of a true theology, vestiges of the thought and holy toil of God-commissioned and God-directed men, and these priceless things must be cherished. The worship and experience and prophesyings of a millennium and a half had cultivated wonderful instincts and aptitudes for spiritual verities into the Jewish temperament. Jesus would not have been the incarnation of the Divine wisdom if He had passed by unnoticed the providential preparation of the past. In spite of the dark and perplexing outlook, every contemporary mind had passed at some time or other through a stage of religious susceptibility, and had been under Divine training. Perhaps it was in youth when the heart was tender and fervent, or under the reading of the Scriptures in the synagogue when some passing trouble had chastened into thoughtfulness, or amidst the Psalms and sacrifices of the Temple courts, or out in the wilderness under the vehement appeals of the Baptist. In these Jewish minds Jesus might fairly expect to find holier and more potent memories than amongst the Gentiles. There were chords awaiting the skilful touch of the musician which needed to be created elsewhere. It is something for the mind to be charged with a store of holy associations, reflective, however brokenly, of the great visions of the past; responsive, however faintly, to the large hopes of the future. These things may prove themselves the rudiments of a faith to be in due time recovered and made perfect.

Is there not a principle in the Master's method which should regulate our work and determine the succession of its parts? Missions to the outcasts should be preceded by missions to the churches, which are often composed of formalists and secret backsliders. Jesus preferred a prepared to crude material. The momentary demand amongst Christian workers is for virgin soil, but the fact is ignored that the maximum of productiveness is not found on virgin soils. Aliens and outcasts will be most effectually influenced if the lost sheep of the house of Israel are first sought and restored.

This restriction upon the range of His ministry was determined in part by our Lord's sense of the aggravated doom awaiting a backsliding nation. When the surgeon is called to some scene of disaster, he does not take every case in the order in which he stumbles across it. Neither does he first direct his steps to the spot from which the loudest cry comes, nor bestow his help where the spectacle is most sickening. He judges out of the store of his own trained discernment, and takes in hand the most critical cases first. And in the same way, throughout the whole of His earthly ministry, Jesus devotes Himself to those whose dangers are the most imminent and awful. He cannot turn aside from His special mission to respond to the sob of this torn and bleeding Gentile heart, without an instructive and admonitory protest at least. His love is large, knowing no bounds; but it is preoccupied by yet more desperate problems. Driven though He is by the temper of the ruling classes to the very frontier of Jewish life, He is still setting Himself to work which He thinks of paramount importance. The woes of the Gentile world are vast and poignant, but no contemporary nation is verging towards such disaster as these rebellious children of Abraham; for none had resisted light so intense and holy, misused privilege so rare and gracious, and thrown away opportunity so golden. Heathen nations on every side were groaning under the pride and selfishness of despots, the gloom and oppression of superstitions, more terrible in their fantastic cruelties even than ruthless absolutisms and the havoc and carnage of chronic war; but their burdens were light compared with the woes which were settling down upon the life of backsliding Israel. Here where such age-long grace had been lavished the peril was supreme, and Jesus could scarcely turn aside to touch with His own hand the dark enigmas of Gentile life. His very kinsmen were drifting into final separation from God, and all the unknown and incurable bitterness involved in that condition. He must set Himself to save at least the salvable portion of the race. And herein lies a lesson for all His followers. The man who leaves God's family to sin is marked out for extraordinary pains and penalties. Directly and indirectly Jesus affirms that punishment has its degrees. The apostate meets the wrath which falls upon men to the uttermost.

Jesus concentrated His ministry upon the Jew to vindicate His Father's faithfulness. Those whom He primarily addressed were a chosen people, the heirs in a peculiar sense of the Covenant promises. Through them the blessing promised to their forefathers was to come upon the great family of man. And the Covenant had been renewed to successive generations. By birth, by circumcision, by the sprinkling of blood, by all the manifold rites of the Temple, they had been brought into sacred federation with the Most High. And God's word could not be lightly set aside. If that word is to be fulfilled only to a believing remnant, Jesus must be the more careful to leave those who are rejected without excuse, and to magnify His Father's truth and faithfulness. After the lapse of centuries, the promise to Abraham, Isaac, and Jacob must be still kept in view, and the forfeited birthright of privilege offered to the faithless people again and again. The most conspicuous and honourable ministry the world ever had in it, is devoted to the one task of calling God's rebellious people to repentance, and using every means of fitting them for the perpetual tenure of Covenant blessing. It cannot be other than hard for God to pass sentence of doom upon the children of His believing friend and servant; and Jesus made Himself an evangelist of the circumcision, to show that on His Father's part there was no shadow of change, forgetfulness, failure. If there is to be unbelief, a rejection of the divinely appointed King well-nigh national in the scale of its ingratitude, darkness, dispersion, judicial pain for those to whom better and more honourable things had been pledged, Jesus at least must offer a free forgiveness to His own treacherous slayers, spend Himself in the work of extolling His Father's grace and compassion, and, by seeking the lost sheep of the house of Israel, show to the very last how ready the God of the patriarchs still is to fulfil His ancient oath. It seemed as though the Father's honour were at stake, and to magnify it the great Teacher set before Himself the one aim of recovering to better things a race universally called, but in peril of reprobation. God is peculiarly pledged to those who have once belonged to His household. The promises have acquired a new sacredness as the Holy Spirit has attested them in the secret place of the soul. They mean more to the man who has once appropriated them than to the man who has never had faith, and necessity is thus laid upon the minister of the New Covenant to vindicate the fidelity of the Divine word.

Jesus limited the range of His personal ministry so that He might afterwards show to the entire world how free and all-inclusive is the love He cherishes towards men. He discriminates for a time, but it is in favour of those who are most set against Him. His tenderness goes out in concentrated and life-long word and deed towards those by whose guile, malice, and ingratitude He is one day to die. The inference for after ages is obvious, that if He is pitiful to these He must be pitiful to all. The very limitations of His ministry make it impossible for the Gentile to despair. Caring with unwavering fidelity for the treacherous and ungrateful Jews, He will care also for the Gentile, whose part in the crime of His death was secondary only, and resolvable into a sin of ignorance. The authority and providential counsels of His Father led Him, through all the successive steps of His ministry, with the message of peace upon His lips, to the centres and strongholds of Jewish pride and envy and persecution, so that against this dark moral background there might be more luminously revealed His redemptive compassions to all men. By the solicitude He showed for those who were His own kinsmen according to the flesh, and who proved themselves so wayward and thankless, malignant and implacable, He magnified mercy and longsuffering for the encouragement of all who should afterwards believe on Him to life everlasting.

And the principle which guided Him is not transient. To forgive one who has obstinately backslidden, and proved treacherous to His name and kingdom, makes a larger draft upon His grace than to wash a heathen man from the blood and abomination which defile him, or receive into His fold the brutal and ignorant sot from a great city's outcasts. And because He wishes to magnify His mercy before the world and win its hope and trust, He seeks first those who need the largest measures of His pity and help, just as in His earthly ministry He sought the lost sheep of the house of Israel. To restore one who has turned back after knowing the way of life, needs the great miracle of pardoning love; and because He seeks to work such miracles still, He concentrates thought, and care, and longing upon those who have put themselves into the extreme of peril, and need the largest share of His redeeming compassions.

CHAPTER VII.

THE UNIVERSAL NOTE IN CHRIST'S TEACHING.

ALTHOUGH our Lord addressed Himself more immediately to the Jews, and was loyal to the local limitations which the counsels of His Father had for the time being placed upon His work, it was an evangel broad as the world He was sent to preach. It is impossible to read those selections from His message which have been handed down to us without being made to feel that He Himself meant its great principles to reach all men without distinction of race or century. The after generations have rightly come to look upon His discourses as directed to universal man, and charged with both threat and promise of world-wide applicability.

Peter once asked, "Speakest Thou this parable unto us, or even unto all?" A startling forecast of our Lord's Second Coming and its issues was the immediate occasion of the question put by the impulsive disciple. In two companion parables the Master had been forecasting the destinies of watchful and unwatchful servants. The returning Lord would Himself minister in acts of unbounded graciousness to those whom He should find vigilant and zealous, whilst to dull and supine servants the Second Advent should be disastrous as the visit of the cunning and ruthless thief. It has been assumed by some that Peter's question referred to the first, and by others to the second parable. The two parables are substantially one, setting forth the same essential fact in widely opposite aspects, so it is immaterial which of the two parables was in Peter's thought. His question implies, Do not the threats apply to the crowd, and are not the promises the special perquisites of those who have long followed Thee? We cannot surely be spoken of in the same breath with promiscuous outsiders? The caustic and the fire are for those who have not joined themselves to the disciples, and the honey and the balm for the inner circle!

Our Lord's reply is indirect, but none the less forcible and impressive on that account. No ordination to office in the kingdom is final. The investiture may be revoked; and if the authority once conferred is to outlast the ages, there must be sustained faithfulness. And, on the other hand, the nameless man in the crowd may be found to have reached the highest distinction at the coming of the King. The judgements of the approaching kingdom deal with character, and not with names and persons and classes as such. For the present the man is masked, and can only be indicated by an interrogation, "Who is the faithful and wise servant?" The question will find its answer in the issues of conduct and after history.

This shrewd spokesman of the Twelve knew that his Master meant some one by the solemnising similitudes He had just used. If the application was not for the Twelve, it must have been for the outside crowd; and if not for the outside crowd, it must have been for the Twelve. It was not Christ's habit to spend time and strength in impersonal disquisitions. Human teachers sometimes discuss subjects which interest themselves only, and have little or no relevance to their hearers; but this Teacher was no mere curious investigator or theoretical educationist. He had not come to sharpen men's wits only, and discipline them to the use of abstract logic: His doctrine was all application, and the truth interested Him, not because of the intellectual exercises to which its problems allured the thinker, but because of its relation to living souls. The art of dealing with abstract principles has its value: He had no time, however, for anything but the most concrete forms of teaching. He never once opened His lips to satisfy curiosity merely, because He had more vital work to do. His preaching was neither vague on the one hand, so that the most sensitive could go away untouched, nor so narrowly personal on the other, that the gossips could say, " He was aiming at our chief scribe to-day." He kept in view, as He taught, definite groups and classifications of character. His discourse was the channel by which the soul-healing virtue of His own personality passed into those whom He addressed. He Himself was the Word, the Word of Life to all mankind, and the message that passed His lips reflected Himself. A universal Saviour, such as He felt Himself sent to be, could not speak impersonal words, or words of limited application only.

Peter, perhaps, might have a colourable pretext for his question, inasmuch as in earlier parables the specific interpretation had been kept for the private ear of the disciples. It was in no temper of exclusiveness, however, that the Teacher adopted this course, but because the

Twelve at that stage were expected to have a little more illumination than the multitude. To assume that all menace was for the outside world, and all encouragement the strict monopoly of the Twelve, was a grave reflection upon the impartiality of Jesus Christ. No such question could have been asked after the great doctrine of universal redemption by the cross had dawned upon the disciples.

That study of the historical setting of the gospel, characteristic of recent years, brings with it an intellectual temptation, and makes men forget the illimitable applications of Christ's teaching. An intent and continuous survey of the outward incidents of the ministry in Galilee and Judea may almost disqualify the modern thinker from fixing his thought upon the permanent and catholic motives of that ministry. A scrutiny is brought to bear upon the underlying history, geographical surroundings, and local atmosphere of the gospel which is almost microscopic. Aided by the ripe results of travel, scholarship, and modern research, we have been brought to realise the scenery through which the Prophet of Nazareth moved, and the circumstances into which He was daily brought. We see Him in the carpenter's shop, and know every primitive tool He used. We cast our glance upon Him seated in the fisherman's boat, or on the mountain side, or under one of the Temple colonnades, and can describe the garments He wore, the attitudes He assumed, the movements of His eye as He turned to His questioners. The conditions of the different disciples is vividly pictured to us, and we are quite at home with the temperaments He had to subdue and to sanctify. All the local colour is restored, and we forget the immense vistas of the background and the wider horizons of Christ's teaching. A Syrian Prophet stands before us, instructing a band of friends and travelling companions, and we half think He had no care for the souls of those who did not wear an Eastern head-dress and a flowing abba. So vividly, and with such wealth of detail, have His life and work been dramatised for us by the poet-biographers of popular theology, that it eludes our perception for the moment that we ourselves form part of His audience, and that His steady, far-discerning gaze searches into our souls and reads their needs as He speaks. Study from the historical standpoint only, narrows the survey. We look for immediate fulfilments of His prophetic forecasts, and assume that the augury is exhausted of its import when the first dawn of a fulfilment has come into view. The judgements of His parables are judgements upon contemporary nations. Gehenna was a valley for refuse just outside Jerusalem, and it is a question whether Jesus taught anything the present century need study upon the subject of retribution. His missionary commission was an injunction to the Twelve, and gives no sanction for the enterprises of the modern Church. We may be Christians without cherishing quixotic enterprises for the conversion of the Mantchoo and the Andaman islander. Crosses and abnegations were for the Twelve, but it is a nineteenth-century duty to seek one's own comfort and physical well-being. And so, under the cover of reverently studying the human factors in the ministry of our Lord, we provincialise His message, and try to fold the universal into a miserable nutshell. His audiences were made up of those who wore raiment of a different colour and pattern from our own, who used a foreign speech and observed dissimilar manners and customs. The parables and the other parts of His message were for His immediate contemporaries rather than for us and for all.

It is scarcely just to transfer to Jesus Christ the limitation and cramped outlook of even the best human teacher. When we speak we cannot penetrate, unless in a very vague way, beyond the twos and threes immediately addressed. We are most moved to those who stand grouped within our immediate circle; and when we endeavour to speak to the many who flit like thin shadows behind the semi-transparent haze which overarches our life, our words become cold, colourless, unpointed. Our sympathy is attenuated by diffusion, and it is a dreamy make-believe when we aspire to make our voices reach those who are not our contemporaries.

It is easy to argue from those ripe conceptions of our Lord's Divine Personality and Sonship which the Church afterwards formulated, to the universality of His message; but can we see in His own mind, character, and consciousness, as reflected in the records of His life and teaching, any sign of the fact that He was speaking to universal man?

The strict and never-failing impartiality of character distinctive of Jesus Christ is clear proof of the universal aim in His teaching. Whilst He claimed the right to choose His helpers and associates, and announced the unchanging conditions of admission to His kingdom, He never selected His audience. He addressed Himself first to the Jews, but recognised from the very beginning that His message in its deepest intention was for every man who had a soul to respond to it. He had no esoteric mysteries in reserve for the Twelve. In His soul-vexing controversies with the Jews He looked wistfully out upon the Gentile adherents of coming days. He prayed, when upon the threshold of His passion, for those who should believe through the disciples' word; and in the hour of His triumphant ascension laid down the charter which secured gospel rights and privileges to far-off lands. Every preferential interest in Christ's teaching was excluded by the justice of His instincts, the spaciousness of His outlook, and His profound consciousness of the fact that He had been sent as the instrument and messenger of a common salvation. In the fullest sense of the term He was without either prejudice or partiality; and to be without prejudice and partiality as a teacher is more than to be so as a minister of the law. He had no kindness for the men of one epoch and indifference to the men of another, no outmelting pity for the ills of a pure-blooded Eastern race and straitened commiseration for the ills of mixed Western races, no effusive help for favoured sections of the population and refusals for less favoured sections, no saving absolutions for transgressors of one shade and unalterable anathemas for sinners of a darker and less fashionable shade. He did not condone faults in those nearest to Him, or overpaint the delinquencies of those from whom He chanced to be widely sundered. He came as an impartial corrector of character and an impartial almoner of redemptive blessing, always looking at men through the counsels of His Father's love, and never through that atmosphere of likes and dislikes which is so prone to gather about our eyes. Comfort and correction were administered without any respect of persons, and the disciple who thought promises were specially intended for the Twelve and threatenings for the multitude, had little sense of the wholeness of his Master's plans and the many-sided sympathies of His character.

Jesus Christ had no sympathy with the temper which had led the founders and advocates of some of the earlier religious philosophies to divide their teaching into esoteric and exoteric portions. He who would monopolise the hopes and promises of the evangel for himself and his class, and turn every threatening upon the unregenerate crowd, is either self-complacent to the point of Pharisaism or drunk with the pride of office, and both these things encountered the severest reprobation from Jesus Christ. The question, " Speakest thou this parable unto us, or even unto all?" implied that a leaven of supercilious exclusiveness was at work in Peter and his fellow-disciples. The Master had shown not a little favour, sympathy, and encouragement to His chosen companions, and it was but human nature to assume that these things had been vouchsafed to them in recognition of their sincerity, self-sacrifice, devotion. The Master who was smiling upon them now would continue to smile as a lasting tribute to their excellencies of character. There was little or no sense of that law of grace to which they owed everything they had; and grace is essentially impartial, and shapes itself into a universal message. Jesus Christ's protest against the ritual of His day was required not only by the fact that it was associated with formalism, insincerity, and death, but no less because it tended to separatism and was hostile to the genius of a world-wide evangelism. And this pride of calling led on to the assumption that office was the recompense of meritorious service, and that office must necessarily bring exemption from those scathing pains and privations sometimes held over the heads of obdurate hearers. Just as in the kingdom of this world rank brought with it immunity from the more extreme inflictions of the penal code, so is it assumed it should be with high estate in the kingdom of God. No possibility of overthrow and doom is before the apostolate. But the Great Teacher hints that the Twelve need to be solemnly admonished as well as the common crowd. The traditions of worldly governments will be reversed in God's household, and "he who knew the Master's will, and did it not, is to be beaten with many stripes." The impartial character of Jesus compels Him to make the threatenings and promises of His parables equally unlimited in their possible applications.

Jesus carried Himself throughout His public ministry like one swayed by the strong persuasion that He had been equipped as a Teacher for all time. The political speeches of one century have little interest save as literary curiosities for the men of the next. Such speeches deal with local and temporary problems that may admit of many solutions, and every fresh generation claims the right of taking its own independent course in dealing with the questions that face it. Very few of the sciences can claim finality, for every department of science does not rest upon a basis of pure mathematics. Inadvertent egotism biases the most honest investigator, and he instinctively desires to put some personal mark upon his own particular branch of study. Constant debate and revision are necessary to eliminate these causes of error and impermanence. In the canons of art, music, and poetry there is more or less of change, all such things being influenced by a fashion which passeth away. Now, it was not without deliberate intent that Jesus set Himself to exclude all geographical and temporal elements from His teaching. He was a patriot, and primarily addressed Himself to His own countrymen, but there was no political tinge in His teaching. He refused to touch matters which belonged to either the local or imperial courts of jurisdiction. He never attempted to treat those quasi-scientific questions which must have fascinated many contemporary minds; for He knew the times were not ripe for a final science, and the most thoughtful work of that age must prove itself impermanent. He separated religion from the ritual with which through centuries it had been associated in Jewish thought; for He knew that inasmuch as for many minds and many races teaching by rite and ceremony was an offence against the dignity of the intellect, a religion of which ritual was an essential constituent could never have the note of universality. There were no two sides to what He taught. The fugitive and the mutable were scrupulously kept out of His message. He gathered His lessons in the realms of the eternal. The doctrine of which He was the exponent could not perish, because it comprised the principles ruling in that deathless realm out of which He had come as a pilgrim. "My word shall not perish." His pronouncement was final. It was the consciousness He had of bringing a message directed to all, that led Him to assert the unrestricted diffusiveness of the truth, "Neither do men light a candle and put it under a bushel," and at a later stage to declare in a majestic anticipation of His boundless spiritual dominion, "I am the light of the world."

To the mind of our Lord each man addressed was typical of others, and He had such wealth of discerning sympathy in His nature, that the one who stood before Him formed a link of association in His rapid thought with all who shared the self-same needs. He saw the multitude in the moral sample with which He was dealing, and those to whom He spake on hillside or in temple court represented practically unlimited classes. Just as the patriarchs who possessed the gift of prophecy looked upon the founder of a tribe or nation, and saw in his personal traits forecasts of the character and fortune of the generations springing from him: so Christ saw the men of all ages classified according to those moral affinities and associations recapitulated in the crowd which encircled Him. We are told that the eyes of insects are made up of tens of thousands of facets or prisms set at varying angles, and that, though one image is probably represented to the brain of the insect, tens of thousands of images are mirrored upon these different facets of the eye. If such an illustration may be used without irreverence and incongruity, an inverted order of that phenomenon seems to illustrate Christ's way of looking at things. His outward eye scans the faces of those to whom He is speaking, but countless images start up within His inner consciousness. Through those in the crowd who had sins to be forgiven, faults to be rebuked, fears to be dispelled, open wounds to be healed, and moral perils calling for His presence as an effectual shield of defence, He saw universal man. It was perhaps by this process He took upon Himself the sin of the race and became its common Redeemer, and the process could scarcely fail to influence Him as a Teacher. In Nathanael He saw inquirers who are a compound of both candour and prejudice; in Simon, the man of impulse, prone to error but quick to repent; in Thomas, the pessimist and the intermittent sceptic; in John, the follower of pure and passionate love; in Zaccheus and the woman who was a sinner, the outcasts of society for whom He shed His blood, and to whom He brought the message of forgiveness; in the Greeks standing in the Temple courts, the earnest of a Gentile world drawn to penitence and worship by His cross; in Jerusalem, destined to speedy doom, a microcosm of the last all-inclusive judgement. The apparent confusion in the discourse, that perplexing interweaving of the near and the distant, may be explained by the fact that He was looking upon both events from one common mental focus. Wherever He taught He saw audiences large as mankind to be smitten and helped by His word; and if there is anything in common between us and those He addressed, His message is direct from His heart to ours.

The words of the Lord Jesus must have been universalised by the sense He had of the world-wide outlook of that sacrifice with which He was to consummate His life. If the death was meant for all, the teaching which prepares men to receive its benefits and to interpret its grace must be likewise meant for all. And in the human nature, which it was Christ's purpose to redeem and to save, there was need for all sides of the Great Teacher's message. The possibilities of human character in both the upward and downward direction were practically illimitable. No term could be put either to the improvement or to the degeneration of which the self-same man was capable. In every man there were faculties which gave promise of good, to the elevation of which no impassable line could be put; and as the complement of that, there was a proclivity to evil which was just as immeasurable in the opposite direction, and the same man needed the sobering and solemnising admonitions which gave such sternness at times to Christ's ministry, and the high encouragements He bestowed upon those out of whose lives all hope had passed. He reminds the Jews that they possess no immunity from the punishment which attends sin, and intimates they are about to share the sharpest penalties which alight upon Gentile transgression. And He reminds His own disciples again and again that they may perchance come to share in the punishment of their reprobate countrymen. They, no less than Israel of old, need to hear both the blessings and the curses of the law. "What I say unto you I say unto all: watch." The disciples are made of common clay, and Peter needs vigilant prayer as much as Judas. And, on the other hand, He stimulates the disciples with promises which to cold unbelief must have seemed fantasy and extravagance. To show that there is no limit put to the application of His word, He makes even His own death, which is a thing apart in its virtue and saving significance, represent principles binding upon all the disciples. He does not deny that there may be right-hand and left-hand thrones in His kingdom, but He repudiates the idea that those thrones may be given capriciously, and otherwise than as the recompense of faithful and patient suffering. His own persecutions suggested the disciples'. And He associates the patient disciples with Himself in His consummated glory, thus showing that in every direction His promises have not cast-iron terms of application.

It was one of the marks of Paul's catholicity, that whilst he preached a world-wide gospel of love and forgiveness, he submitted himself to the threatening of Christ's word. He was stirred by the fear lest, after having preached the gospel to others, he himself should become a castaway. Unlike Peter at the earlier stage of his training, he never assumed the promises were for the saints and the threatenings for the crowd of outside sinners. One sometimes wonders if Luke, who records the parables replying to Peter's question, and setting forth the perils of those who fill office in the Church of Christ, had reported the incident and the conversation to which it gave rise to Paul. If so, Paul must have been under the influence of those reflections when he confessed the need he had for discipline and watchfulness lest he himself should be numbered at last with the outcasts. He recognises, as did Jesus Christ, that no line of distinction can be drawn in applying the Divine message. In all its parts it is a message for all, and those who are to be presented perfect in Christ Jesus must be both "warned" and "taught." No past attainment can exempt from wrath, no rank in the Church can confer immunity from terrible judgement when lawlessness of temper and conduct break out. The most highly-placed servant shall be cut asunder and have his portion with the hypocrites. The presence of Judas in the inner circle proved that the apostolate itself needed the solemn note of warning, and the after-admission of Paul to the apostolate proved that the man in the crowd was as much concerned in the magnificent promises which fell from the lips of the Great Teacher as the chief apostle or the beloved disciple himself.

CHAPTER VIII.

COUNSELS AGAINST WORLDLY CARE.

WORLDLY care is commonly looked upon as one of the minor sins of human nature, if indeed it is to be accounted a sin at all, and yet Jesus warned men against it perhaps more frequently than against any of the specific offences current in His time. His answer to the tempter, "Man shall not live by bread alone, but by every word that proceedeth out of the mouth of God," shows that His thought had been early drawn to this grave moral peril, and that He had already guarded Himself against this popular and dominant spiritual transgression. In calling the Twelve into personal association with Himself and His work, He makes it one of His primary conditions that they should break loose from the secular entanglements of the past; and when He sends them forth upon their first separate venture as His messengers, He warns them in startling terms against solicitously prearranging the ways and means of livelihood. And these counsels, against what worldly minds would esteem necessary prudence, He repeats to the Seventy who are commissioned to be His heralds in one of the closing stages of His ministry. These at least whom He directly authenticates must be patterns of aloofness from the selfish struggle of the world, and must not in any degree suffer their hearts to be eaten out by temporal cares. The first and second miraculous draft of fishes are intended to give them courage in carrying out this lesson. The parable of the Sower in the mid-period of our Lord's ministry, and that of the Marriage Feast at the close, both show how sadly sensible He was to the fact that worldly cares were constantly shutting men out from the benefits of the gospel. In the synagogue at Capernaum the great Teacher had before Him a feverish multitude of men and women, smitten right and left with this grovelling temper as with some dire epidemic, and He had to tell them plainly that they sought Him because their minds were possessed with sordidness, and that whilst such was the case it was impossible for them to appreciate the spirituality of His message. The rich young ruler and the sanguine scribe who wished to be admitted to personal discipleship, till he heard of the hardships in the Master's lot, must have been typical of thousands and of tens of thousands who were kept back, not so much by flagrant vices as the spirit of worldliness. Even Martha, good and devoted disciple though she was, could not pass to the high vantage-ground reached by her sister, because she was cumbered with the cares incident to her open-hearted hospitalities. The counsels against anxiousness, which took shape in the memorable reference to the ravens and the lilies, have a place both in the Sermon on the Mount and in an exhortation to the disciples immediately following the story of the Rich Fool. The words in this later context have an accent of peculiar solemnity, intimating, as they do, that a man may make final shipwreck of the soul through this sin of worldly foreboding and solicitude. Rich and poor are victims alike. It may seem more excusable in the poor, but it is perhaps even more common in the rich, from whom our Lord takes His specific examples. Few men are harassed to the point of insanity as our millionaires. That which the modern doctor describes as overstrain and nervous exhaustion, the bold, heart-searching Speaker of the story of the Rich Fool intimates is unpardonable sin against which the swift and capital sentence of Divine justice has gone forth.

Every age has some apology to make for its own special besetments, and our Lord's contemporaries could doubtless have made out as plausible an apology for themselves as the men upon whom the burdens of a new civilisation are pressing. The Jewish State was admirably conceived in the beginning to minimise the evil of economic competition, and reduce pauperism to that trivial residuum which is produced by accident and calamity. Life was simple, and every man had his inheritance, from which he could not be permanently dislodged by the arts of usury and land-jobbing. With the developments of home and foreign trade in the time of Solomon, a new temper of restlessness and ostentation seems to have inoculated the national character. The Captivity checked for a time the temper of growing worldliness, and upon the return there was a transient revival of that kind, idyllic equality of life aimed at in the first settlement of the land. But the later conquests, besides infecting many of the people with the secular temper of the conquerors, gave rise to a new class of fears. No country becomes richer by its subjection, and the spectre of poverty began to haunt many a Jewish home. The least outbreak of impatience against the Roman yoke might bring to an end the scant measure of freedom and prosperity still left to them. Prudent men may have been naturally exercised by sad thoughts of their future and that of their children.

But the temper against which the Master warned is not, after all, the product of special economic or political conditions. It is chronic in human nature, and is the offspring of greed, pride, scepticism. Every age is tempted to strain to an over-eager secularism, to those sordid cares and solicitudes which clasp their tentacles about the heart and strangle out its best and noblest life.

Jesus Christ came as a Friend of humanity to raise society to a higher level of well-being, and it grieved Him to find men's hearts eaten out by forebodings which concerned the mere fringe of existence. With that unerring insight which always characterised Him, He saw that here lay the root of not a little of the world's misery and suffering. It was then, and is still, the direct cause of many diseases; and He who can give men escape from their fears will heal many of the maladies, not only of His own, but of succeeding generations likewise. The fancy of one who lacks faith is a tyrant dark and terrible as those who ride roughshod over the nations. Cares and anxieties are the Kurds and Bashi-Bazouks of the brain, and they enact atrocities just as dreadful as those which curdle the blood of the good Christians who read of them. It would need a large asylum, indeed, to shelter those who are broken down and wofully wrecked by the needless burdens they have taken upon their hearts. The plain facts of existence are sometimes hard and grim enough in themselves, but gloomy sentiment and imagination, unbalanced by faith in God's providential sovereignty, clothe with quite unnecessary terror the sombre realities of the world in which we struggle. A wise political economy must deal with the poverty and privation in our midst, but material palliatives applied in the most skilful and ungrudging fashion will not heal this inward derangement. If perfect equality could be achieved, and the State could own all the instruments of production, rival States would compete with each other just as recklessly as the greediest capitalists; and if even the whole world could be put under one central government of absolute impartiality, we should begin to think of the time when the sun's heat will be exhausted and the planet reduced to a chemical refuse-heap. The disease is in men, and can no more be cured by the expedients of a perfectly equal civilisation, than the craze of the millionaire who thinks he is fated to die in a poorhouse can be cured by the present of a purse of golden guineas.

Those who are least likely to feel the pinch of privation are often melancholy specimens of the destructive tendency of worldly care. This temper, which the Great Teacher diagnosed with such skill, is in our character rather than in our environment, and, like the seed of some hereditary disease, unless jealously watched and counteracted, will sooner or later make itself felt. Secret shadows are brought upon human life everywhere by this mood of mind against which Christian disciples are warned. It is a quite unnecessary penance we lay upon ourselves, and the worst of it is, this spiritual disease is of an infective type. We cannot be anxious without stirring up in others the same mental torment. The great Friend of humanity hates all needless pain. He who sometimes asks His servants to undertake sharp and heroic sacrifices for the sake of others, never wishes them to inflict gratuitous unhappiness upon their own souls. Care never made a burden the lighter or helped the solution of a practical perplexity, and yet the victims of care outnumber those of disease; and, but for the folly and guilt of their unbelief, are perhaps more to be pitied. The Divine Son of Consolation would fain give men relief from this dull, stubborn pain, this monotonous heart-ache, this self-tormenting and cancerous temper of soul.

This down-dragging preoccupation of mind was *the chief difficulty our Lord had to face as a religious Teacher*. There were times and seasons when the multitudes gathered about Him, but they were drawn by the fame of His miracles rather than by interest in the lessons He taught. Into the minds of some of them He could scarcely work an idea edgeways. It was only from the few that He gained an earnest and intelligent hearing. The serious thinker has no chance in a busy, feverish, self-occupied age. Men will consent to forget their cares in amusements only, and they demand as an antidote to their grey, week-day thoughts a sensationalism fierce as dram-drinking. The inimitable word of Him into whose lips grace had been poured could not find entrance into the distracted minds around Him, unless He could teach His hearers the art of forgetting the world and its engrossing interests. Men must dismiss the trifles which are engaging their lower faculties before the higher half of the being can be quickened and brought into play. What a disheartenment it must have been to One who had come from afar with a great and inconceivably beneficent message upon

His lips, to find men's minds so stubbornly preoccupied. The angel of emancipation had come into the gloom of the prison-house to proclaim the acceptable year of the Lord, but the half-demented captive was so bent upon counting the stones of his cell, and finding omens in the study of its lichens and cobwebs, that he was unconscious of the delivering presence. Some gleam of a better life has kindled itself within men when they will consent to drop for a time their thoughts of earthly things. This is the faith which must be mixed with the hearing of the Word if it is to profit as God in His great-heartedness intends it.

The Divine Son came as a pattern and an apostle of faith, and the anxiety against which He admonishes is the sworn enemy of faith in all the forms of its application. Faith must first assert itself through the facts of the natural life, and then it will be prepared to assert itself through those larger facts of the spiritual life about which He had been sent to speak. Men not infrequently profess a large confidence in the promise of the life to come, who treat the present life as though it were a chaos of anarchic confusion and struggle, out of which a controlling God had been finally cast out. By oppressive forethought and struggle, suicidal in its distressfulness, men claiming to be religious seem to think they must needs insure themselves against the evil chances of life, just as the possessors of silver and jewellery insure against burglars. They treat hoards, bank balances, investments, and real estate as though they were earthworks to defend weak places in God's guardianship. It is one of their foundation principles that life is and ever must be a fierce and a relentless struggle, and they take their part in making and keeping it so. They act upon the assumption, not that a benign prodence reigns, but that the gladiatorial show enters into God's method of government, and that they please God by taking part in the frantic and unrelenting contest. Till that unconfessed but deeply-rooted error is removed, men can neither have that faith in God which is required from His children, nor that kind and equable temper towards each other which is one of the fruits of faith. The Great Teacher of faith needed to get this portentous stumbling-block out of the way before He could effectually bring home and enforce His lesson.

Jesus came as a Saviour from sin, and He saw and felt that *the care against which He so repeatedly admonished men was at the root of not a little of the world's transgression.* Some sins are begotten by our primary passions, but others take their rise in those secondary passions which are bred of worldly solicitude. The niggard, the miser, the oppressor of the poor, the spoiler of the rich, the trafficker in vice and corruption, are manufactured out of this raw material. It is this mood of anxiety which leads the man made for better things to take hold of the muck-rake with a death-grip which never relaxes. Undue thought of the body makes the majority of our fellow-citizens shut up their compassions from the holiest charities which invite their help. It tempts men to hoard that which will only prove a curse to themselves and their children, and might otherwise be made a gracious service to the community. It is this which sometimes allures the man to peculation who has all that heart could wish. Here lies the tap-root of the difficulty between capital and labour. Men on both sides of the question are weighted by this nightmare, and speak and act in ways unworthy of their best selves. It is this which makes some men surly, reserved, and insular. They are disinclined to friendship, lest they should be constrained to show themselves friendly in the terms of the national currency. It is this habit of undue care which makes the rich fool, and leaves him planning new barns and storehouses whilst men faint with hunger around him, and the angel is speeding mid-heaven to execute the

Divine decree. No wonder the Great Teacher was accustomed to speak more frequently against this unhappy temper of mistrust than against many specific forms of sin, for from this subtle and widely-diffused germ almost every form of sin may grow. It is opposed both to the love of God and man. It is the inclined plane leading down into the dreariest possible atheism of thought. It was the besetting and fundamental sin of Gehazi, Iscariot, Ananias, and Demas, who went back to the world. Then, as now, it had a significantly close relation to the loss of the soul. Our Lord could save men from the dominion of sin only by saving them from their cares.

Our Lord came not merely to teach, comfort, and save men, but *to enlist and equip them for higher service than had yet been rendered to the world*, but He could not make them all He intended them to be till He had first taught them the secret of a free mind. They were disqualified by the fearfulness and distraction of their common life; for worldly care is inconsistent with complete consecration to the Divine service. Men can no more fight God's battles whilst they are unduly exercised about the questions of the bodily life, than an ill-fed soldier, sent on his campaign by a bankrupt government and burdened with a hundredweight of baggage, can successfully fight the battles of his country. There can be no wholeheartedness where this heathenish temper of worldly solicitude is ever fretting the life. Jesus had come to set up a kingdom whose citizens were to be characterised by unexampled liberality; but he who is haunted by thoughts about the food and raiment of to-morrow, can never be open-handed. Our Lord had come to create a new generation of thinkers; but there can be no steady contemplation of the mysteries of God by the man who is over-careful about the mere accidents of the temporal life. The Son of God wanted workers for His holy enterprises in the midst of the world; but there can be no intense and self-forsaking toil, and no grand co-partnership in the work of the eternal, where men are haunted by the petty trifles of time. It was His aim to organise human life into a gigantic and world-wide philanthropy; but secular solicitude was inseparable from spiritual paralysis. Men must have free minds if they are to be full of love to God and man; and the reverse is equally true, that they must be full of that love of God which is vitally associated with faith, if they are to find escape from galling burdens of care. The only effectual remedy for harassment and distraction is to get the mind occupied by higher and better things. It is a popular impression that men can emancipate themselves from care by any act of faith in the Divine providence, without giving themselves body and soul to the work of the Redeemer's kingdom. But to inspire serenity by His assuring message, so that men might live more pleasantly to themselves than in the troubled and perplexing past, was not the end of the Great Teacher's message. He did not come to do the work of those modern companies which give men ease of mind by insuring their investments. He did not teach so that men might attain a more happy-go-lucky mood of soul in their worldly pursuits and avocations.

The mind will inevitably turn to the old cares, unless its powers are fully employed upon the nobler pursuits He sets before it. If we are to learn this Christlike tranquillity, and enter into the heritage of His matchless peace; if this life of untroubled song like that of the birds, this ideal of calm, silent beauty like that of the blowing lilies, is to be ours,—we must be servants of the kingdom. Men sometimes excuse themselves from active participation in the work of the Church, on the ground that they have so many business cares, worries, irritations. The best anodyne against worldly fear, vexation, gloomy outlook is not sleep, for dreams themselves may be as troubled as Pharaoh's, but service in the Redeemer's kingdom. We must yield ourselves to the fascination of higher subjects and pursuits, since that is the only remedy against the ills which oppress the brain. The activity of discipleship is a part of the Master's prescription against care.

The fact that in separating ourselves to God's service we have left the world and its cares behind us, will help our faith. Men have no right to expect the countless benefits of God's guardianship, unless they are playing their divinely appointed part in the kingdom. A Chinese gambler, when asked to forsake his sin, and assured that the God who fed the birds would take care of him if he would only have courage to do the right, replied, "The birds steal, and I am not quite so bad as that." But is it true? As God judges things, the birds have their rights, and are not thieves. They exercise the same defence over the farmer's interests that David and his followers exercised over the flocks of Nabal, and have claim to tribute. They deliver the crops from a thousand pests, and God brings a swift retribution upon the lands where they are wantonly destroyed. We can ill afford to spare the most troublesome of them. They do their part. And the lilies have their right to sun and soil. They brighten many a dull nook of the world, and both by their beauty and their symbolic teaching they justify their title to a place in the soil. The rude soul of a peasant has some reverence for the bloom, and would think it sacrilege to treat it as he treats the thistle when he passes by with spud or scythe. The loveliness into which it expands is its armour of defence. And so with the man who is filling his place and doing his work in the providential sphere where God has put him. No wonder men sometimes feel anxious about their own future and that of their children. They are cumberers of the ground, living selfishly themselves, and training their children to selfish and luxurious views of life, and do nothing to justify the care which God's providence exercises over those who have the Spirit and do the work of His Son. If we are in right paths we shall get what God wills us to get, and His will is good. We are perhaps better without some of the things upon which we have set our foolish and selfish hearts.

A critic of our Lord's teaching once said that His views of Divine providence were a distinct incitement to thriftlessness, but the critic must surely have been both wanting in appreciation of the true drift of the teaching, and blind to the deep maladies of our social life. Care is an enemy of true industry, and it is no reckless or indolent temper which Jesus intends to foster. Care is the friction which wastes power, accelerates decay, and hampers the productiveness of human toil. Some years ago, a famous mathematician and scientist told the self-opinionated manufacturers of one of our large towns that their machinery made far too much noise. It was a loss of power. Probably they have learned wisdom by the hint an outsider gave them since those days. When the clatter and roll of machinery shakes mills and factories to their very foundations, the manufacturer is not getting the maximum result for what he spends. When men are hot and tremulous with secular anxiety, when they do their work under conditions of fiercest strain, when they are so seething with distractions that they resent giving a moment's thought to any subject outside the immediate groove of business, not only are they wearing themselves into the grave, but they are doing less effective work from the worldly standpoint than they would compass if they would learn Christ's lesson. Faith in providence helps all sides of our life, making us better workers in our common calling, and worthier servants of the kingdom of God's Son.

CHAPTER IX.

THE SOWER AND THE GALILEAN OUTLOOK.

THE inference is probably correct which assigns the lake-side parables to the first stage in our Lord's waning popularity; for they seem to reflect the discouragements which characterised His later ministry in the northern province. In the entire group of parables we may see an acknowledgment of the mixed results hitherto attained, as well as an invincible hope that the future of the kingdom and its interests would be vastly brighter and better than the past.

Three causes of failure are indicated in this carefully elaborated parable. The type represented by the wayside hearer is stolid, impassive, animal,—the man of whom it is sometimes said, with an over-indulgent charity, that he has no capacity for religion and no gleam of interest in its problems. He does not even dabble with it for a time. He disappoints no promise, for the failure dates from the beginning onwards. In the rocky-ground hearer there is superficial intelligence, facile emotion, an incipient advance towards spiritual truth, but complete lack of set purpose and staying power. He is the convert of passing excitement, the impressionable creature of special missions, religious quicksilver ready to scurry into any channels that may be open. The thorny-ground hearer has intelligence, emotion, and some degree of the grit which can defy opposition; but in the long run he also disappoints his early promise, because there has never been that complete renunciation of the world demanded by an absolute and a sovereign faith. He is wanting in single-mindedness, and has taken no step to repair his deficiency. Side by side with the seed of the kingdom the world is stubbornly installed within his heart. In the first case there was no conversion at all; in the second case the conversion was transient; the third category seems to include those who are religious for long, but who backslide at a more advanced period, because of the tempers of worldliness which strangle the promise of the beginning. The fruitful hearer is free from all such shortcomings. He combines the intelligence of the Scot, the quick sensibility of the Gaul, the dogged perseverance of the Teuton, and the single-mindedness of the child.

The lack of saving intelligence shown in the first type is not constitutional. The Great Teacher was not so wanting in just reasonableness as to demand intelligence from the man who was incapable of it. A mental deadness is all too common, which arises not from some misfortune of birth or constitution, but from sloth, neglect, preoccupation with gross and ignoble aims. That stupor which gives rise to the first cause of failure dealt with in the parable, is essentially moral in its basis. The soil of the trampled footpath was just as rich in the elements of fertility as the soil which gave most lavishly to the sickle. Its unfitness and inability to receive and cherish the seed was entirely artificial. The intelligence which is the first step to discipleship and service, and the lack of which is an omen of barrenness and approaching woe, is the intelligence which comes not from natural aptitude or education or culture, but from heedfulness of the conscience, the art and habit of taking pains in the things of God, that temper of deep, devout earnestness which is a sufficient motive-power to energise all the faculties of the soul. Men who are keen of wit and agile in mental movement, and rich in miscellaneous culture, sometimes grow dense and crass when they are face to face with the Word, because they lack that interest in the spiritual which is the spring of all illuminating power.

Doubtless many of the causes which operated to stupefy the mind and unfit it to understand the gospel message, were the same in our Lord's time as in our own. The conquering hosts of Romans, the tax-gatherers and the tyrants of trade and agriculture, the groups of long-robed priests and scribes, the representatives of those coarse games and demoralising pleasures which had come in with the Roman civilisation, all had their share in trampling the bypaths of Jewish life into hardness, and destroying throughout large sections of life all fitness to receive the seed. Or, to drop for a moment the metaphor of the parable, many had become possessed by the dulness and the coarse, sullen Stoicism which often characterise the victims of military and political enslavement. Under the combined influence of foreign conquest, oppressive usury, declining faith, life had put on many of those marks of degradation which characterise the ways of pariah dogs. In some cases crowds followed Jesus Christ, with no gleam of interest in His teaching, but sniffing for the mere pickings of His miracles. They wanted as their Messiah one who would destroy the castle government by aliens in Jerusalem, give them a loaf as cheap as wilderness manna, and fields and vineyards they could dress and till for the benefit of their own families rather than for that of the money-lenders. In some cases they had been driven into shiftlessness, improvidence, animal stupor, by the grinding despotism under which they lay. For the time being they had lost capacity to consider and appreciate the truth. Worship through an official priesthood had done not a little to deaden all sense of the claims of personal religion. The growth of a class of official scribes had led to the assumption that theology was to be left to the learned, and popular thinking upon religious questions was showing a tendency to die out. And amongst some sections of the population a new craze for pleasure and luxury had sprung up, under the example and patronage of the Romans. Many had become unfitted through these causes to understand Christ's message; just as many in our day are unfitted, through the cruel sordidness of our industrial system, the absorbing tendency of competitive business struggle, the claim of sacerdotal churches to discharge a vicarious service for the worshipper, and discourage, if not prohibit, independent religious thought, as well as through the deadening excess of pleasure, even when the pleasure is not in itself vicious. The mind is in many cases so indurated by these influences, that one might as well expect a crop of wheat from a handful of grain scattered in Threadneedle or Lombard Street, as expect religious wakefulness and discernment in those whose best and highest sensibilities have been so utterly deadened.

The parable intimates it is just this failure to understand, which gives the Evil One his power against the heedless hearer of the Word. He who is to enter into the blessings of the kingdom has something more than his natural forgetfulness to reckon with. In every cultivated country, crowds of hungry birds watch round the field where the sower is at work, and, as soon as his back is turned, patter like a hailstorm down into the furrows and pick up every uncovered seed. They are on the alert all the year round, and seem to know how many trailing ears will be caught by the trees as the harvest waggon creeps through the wooded lane, and how many grains will leak out of the sacks which are stood up against each other in the railway truck, and how many intractable strips of soil in the field will make ready for them sumptuous banquets. And the Great Enemy of the kingdom has his representatives nestling round about every assembly of hearers, ready to foil and thwart the mind in its apprehension of the truth. The truth that has entered into our reason and heart is truth of which we can never be robbed. It has no lodging-place in a man's judgement and conscience till he can grasp its essential principles. Neither the putting up of a religious symbol over the field, nor the tinkling of consecrated bell or tomtom, will keep off the birds. The seed can only be made safe, and the soul along with the seed, by getting vital truth into the central faculties of the life. A slight study of the literature of modern infidelity will show that the men who have abjured Christianity, in nine cases out of ten, never knew what Christianity was. When a man begins to ponder deeply Christ's teachings, he is on the highway to salvation. He has at least passed out of the category of wayside hearers. Other causes of failure may arise later on, but the initial impediment is effectually displaced and removed.

The second cause of failure lies a little more below the surface of things than the first. Underneath a sprinkling of soil, too thin for the support of vegetable life, a continuous layer of rock was hiding itself. It would have been possible to remove the film of rock with pick and crowbar, or at least to deepen and improve the overlying soil. The wheat grains falling upon this section of the field give every sign of growth and fruitfulness for a time. Indeed, at the outset, some degree of growth is possible without the help of the soil at all, for nature stores within the husk of the grain itself sufficient nutriment to feed the germ in the earlier stage of its evolution. If the grain be kept sufficiently moist and warm, it will grow for a few days in the air, but such experiments never increase and cheapen bread. A time comes when the seed must draw, and that largely, upon the resources of the soil. For a time the soil bids fair to respond to the demand made upon it. The green blade appears, and makes uncommonly rapid advances. Indeed, there is something suspicious about this lavish and premature germination. The young wheat plants have an excessive upward development, for there is an impediment to the free extension of the rootlets, and underneath the thin sprinkling of mould there is the bare, inexorable rock. A few days of hot subtropical sun end the brave show, and that which promised much withers away.

In one of his observant nature sketches, the late Richard Jefferies tells how a forgotten ruin was discovered in a meadow from which the grass had just been cut. The summer had been exceptionally hot, and, in the midst of richer and more luxuriant grass, breadths of thin and half-withered grass were seen running in cross and parallel lines, and these strips of ill-favoured growth assumed the form of a ground-plan of church or monastery. Just beneath the surface there ran the courses of massive foundation-stones. There was not enough surface soil resting upon them to retain the moisture through months of protracted drought, and in this way the underlying obstruction was brought into view. The impediment to growth in this case was artificial, but it was of precisely the same character as that the Great Teacher had in view in the second portion of the parable.

The similitude is intended to describe those not uncommon cases in which men are partially touched by the gospel. It has appealed to the poetry or sentiment of their natures, but has not engaged the best powers of the judgement and the conscience. A frequent symptom of the underlying rock is a feverish, over-eager, and ostentatious reception of the truth. Whilst there is a sense in which the acceptance of the evangel cannot be too eager or too rapid, and it is at our jeopardy we postpone its claims, yet there is also a sense in which the assumption of discipleship and its responsibilities may outrun our slow thought and honest, deliberate resolve. The play of emotion, fancy, imagination, is rapid, but acts of judgement are always more or less measured and pauseful. A man speaks in less impetuous terms when his reason is at work, than when his feelings are moved and poetic enthusiasm comes into play. A shallow temperament, made up of surface-conceits and sensibilities, may sometimes respond more swiftly to the truth than a temperament of nobler and more thoughtful cast. Feeling may be too facile, and unless leagued with the other faculties of the soul, it will by and by die out through sheer shallowness. To those who receive the gospel as a sensation, who are romanceful, and are drawn by the picturesque situations it presents, who assume that it ministers to the healthy excitement and hilarity of life, a testing-time is sure to come. Persecution, be it covert and refined or frankly brutal, is not an unmixed evil, if it clearly discover our final limitations and infirmities before the last harvest is at hand.

The type of temperament represented by the rocky-ground hearer is just as common in the secular as in the religious sphere. Many dream pleasantly of worldly success, who have resolutely set themselves against the pain, difficulty, humiliation, which are commonly the conditions for its attainment. Many a man hopes to get rich by a lucky investment or a startling invention, but resents the very mention of toil, patience, long hours, a thousand little economies of self-denial. Perhaps even a dishonourable employment of his wits is a more attractive idea to him than an honourable employment of his hands. He has no arithmetic for difficulties. The literary aspirant expects, like Byron, to wake up some morning and find himself famous, and he resents all study which makes a severer demand upon the brain than novel and newspaper reading. There must be no headaches, no midnight vigils, no devotion to study, when friends invite to gaiety and mirth. The subaltern whispers to some little knot of flatterers, that he expects to be commander-in-chief of the British army, and fumes if he cannot have wines and delicacies in his tent at every stage of the march. The amateur explorer has fixed his eye on the gold medal of the Royal Geographical Society, but the prospect of vegetarian diet for a week would send him back to the coast with an awful story of unexpected horrors to explain his return. The laurel of genuine earthly fame and prosperity can scarcely grow upon such a thin tegument of soil. Wherever there is the underlying rock of unthinking greed and over-pampered softness, the seed of common worldly success cannot strike root downwards and bear fruit upwards.

And it has ever been so in religious things, from our Lord's time down to the present hour. There are not a few who fasten only upon the promises of godliness, and forget its ethic. So intoxicated are they by the idea of receiving, that they ignore the service which is due from them, and the difficult conditions under which that service must often be rendered. The gospel does not educe those possibilities of love, gratitude, self-abnegation which are hidden away somewhere in the character. All pain, trial, sacrifice, should cease with the acceptance of the gospel, and life glow into a perpetual Maytime or June. The ready sensibilities fasten upon the roseate bloom and promise of the evangel, and forecasts of coming tribulation and the demand for unflinching confession are persistently ignored.

This defective spirit is often allied with Pharisaic self-complacency. When the heart has been broken because of sin, men no longer start back before pain and peril. In fact, they do not wish to have a lot that is too soft and luxurious. Having found escape from the terrors of God's wrath, and made their refuge in His infinite tenderness, they are quite willing to be reproached and hated and outlawed of men for the gospel's sake. Paul never declined loss and danger and the many hazards of his troubled career, for the simple reason that his heart had been utterly broken before God, and he had no inclination to make terms with Divine providence for an easy life. When the nature has been subdued and sin bitterly sorrowed for, the seed will be able to put forth strong and deep-reaching roots.

The formalism of service which is allied with self-complacency forms another obstruction to the vigorous germination of the seed. The deadening round of mechanical observances sometimes reasserts itself over the convert, especially when he lacks true conviction of sin; and till a new experience comes to the soul, the essential vitality of the gospel can win no approach into the deepest places of his life. It is the genius of some systems to promote formalism, and yet mill-round externalisms may dominate the adherents of purely spiritual systems. Men satisfy themselves with the letter rather than with the spirit, submitting to an outward precept rather than experiencing the power of an ever-expanding life, reaching a fixed point in religion and never getting beyond it. They are stagnant and not progressive, doting on the mere accidents of a conversion that took place in the distant past, and void of all definite aspirations for the future. Their minds are closed to the deep mysteries which concern the disciple's union with His Master and his full sanctification to the Divine service. The religion they possess only touches a section of the mind's faculties, and that the least noble.

Sometimes this separating rock is the temper of obstinate reservation, which vitiates our surrender to God and our obedience to the claims of His service. We lack wholeheartedness. We feel the charm of the gospel, and are delighted to heed it up to a certain point. But we want to define many of our obligations rather than let the Great Teacher define them for us. Our piety is dreamy, partial, capricious, with a notable lack of rigid, death-defying principle in it.

The people who were carried away by a brief-lived enthusiasm for the miracle-working Prophet, and wished to make Him King forthwith; the impulsive woman who was so enchained by Christ's speech that she broke out into the effusive rhapsody, "Blessed is the womb that bare Thee"; the man who exclaimed, "Master, I will follow Thee whithersover Thou goest," and disappeared from the scene when he heard that his hero was without home or pillow for His weary head; the Galatians whose joy and devotion knew no bounds at the first hearing of the gospel, but who were turning back to seek complete redemption from sin in Jewish rites; the companions of St. Paul who left him to stand alone at his first answer before Cæsar,—all had the defects and the sterilising limitations depicted in the figure of the rocky ground. There was no deep root, no staying power in the time of persecution, for the seed had not as yet touched the richest depths of the soul. Even Peter was in danger of becoming a hearer of this category, when he proposed to draw the line of reasonable forgiveness at seven times rather than at seventy times seven. But for the prayer, "Lord, increase our faith," he would have failed to rise to all the magnanimity and perfection of the gospel. The forgiven debtor, who, after having received his royal master's munificent release from mill-stone bonds, refused to show the slightest fraction of grace to a fellow-servant, was one who received the word in rocky places. Delighted at the thought that the king had cancelled his debt, he broke into words of eloquent eulogy and fair promise. This forgiveness was unprecedented, and the memory of it would make his life a new thing. But the temptation came. It met him on the threshold of his good fortune, and the springing plant withered away, for there was rock in his heart. Some, alas! respond with enthusiasm and ecstasy to the cross whilst it is the instrument that cancels a debt, but let it present itself as a thrice holy symbol of the call to personal devotion, sacrifice, forgiveness, and they turn away with chilled hearts and averted glances. If the gospel is to unfold itself within men in all the grandeur of its unknown potencies, there must be the generous, measureless, unvarying surrender of the whole personality to its spirit. He who is ready to do something in response to the gospel call, but not everything, who has reservations, who locks certain portions of his nature off from the sovereignty of Christ's words, who is willing to do the part but not the whole, belongs to this second category.

It is only within the last generation that the phrases, "natural selection," "the survival of the fittest," "the struggle for existence," have grown up and become familiar to the ear, but the simple facts themselves are as old as the world. It is to the group of processes described by these modern expressions that the Great Teacher glances in the third section of His parable. The competition between the wheat plant and the thorn sets forth the struggle going on in many hearts between the spirit of the world and the simplicity of faith. If strength means fitness to survive, the thorn succeeds in establishing its place and title, whilst the tender wheat plant goes to the wall. Due preparation must be made for the sowing and the thorns must be honestly plucked up by the roots where there is to be a plenteous ingathering. The lackadaisical husbandman who simply lops off the noxious growths of the neglected field, will pay the penalty of his own folly and laziness. He cannot afford to tolerate the law of open competition on his farm. The tender wheat of a few spring days has no chance against the buried, perennial, irrepressible thorn. The thorn can subsist for a time on the scantiest materials and through the bleakest possible conditions, but let it once get the chance, and it annexes all the resources of its frailer and more fastidious neighbours. It gets a double portion of the soil, the sun, and the rain, and never gives a moment's thought or care to the less robust growths of the vegetable kingdom. If the adjacent wheat plants do not get the special help of the man who tills the ground, the greedy, grasping, barbaric thorn will stifle them all.

Thorny-ground hearers are those who have never realised how antagonistic are the claims of

God and Mammon, and who set themselves to find an impossible equation between the two. There can be no compromise between wheat and thorn, and one or the other must give way. It is a clear choice between alternatives that the Master puts before those who would receive His Word. Plants are not unknown in nature which are mutually helpful, and, like Robin Hood and Little John in the old story, further the interest and welfare of each other's lives. But there can be no mutual help or obligation between the spiked despot of the wilderness and the tender growths of the cultivated field. The covert passion of worldliness, when cherished, will prove itself stronger than the delicate spiritual affections which the gospel quickens.

Growths of a different type may be included in this broad popular term "thorns." There are barren thorns,—harsh briers that bear no tinted blooms, mere instruments of miserable cruelty and castigation;—"the cares of this life." All pain and no pomp, much spike and no grace or fragrance,—poignant, obstructive, heart-lacerating solicitudes. Where these exist, religion is growing in the shadow, if it can be called growing at all, perhaps making a forlorn fight for mere existence in the human soul.

And then there are the thorns which

are gay with flowers,—thorns men are even tempted to cultivate for their colour and promise; —" the deceitfulness of riches and the lusts of other things." Harshness is subordinated to luxury, the naked bramble hides itself under brave show and seductive splendour. With growing prosperity, the one care has become not for food and raiment, but how most successfully to multiply existing possessions and enlarge the area of sensuous enjoyment. When wealth once comes, no term can be put to the new passions which spring up within the man and choke the seed.

It is easy to see how worldliness thwarts the growth and manifestation of that love which is unfolded in the soul by the indwelling gospel, for the same temper is hostile to all high human love. Pathetic illustrations present themselves in the homes of the poor and of the rich alike. Where work is ill-paid and precarious, a cloud gathers upon the brow of the wage-earner. The wrongs and mortifications of the outside world find their way into the home, and produce petulance, moroseness, recrimination. And the cares of the over-driven housewife, who has to be mother, cook, nurse, maid-of-all-works in one, and to make a wretched pittance go a very long way in expenditure, produce a fretfulness, a tension, a sense of heart-weight, often fatal to domestic happiness. The anxious and overwrought sufferers in these lives of care reproach each other in their miserable martyrdom, and at last the love of early years fades irrevocably away. The thorn of care overshadows and strangles all that is gracious in domestic sympathy and love.

And the deteriorating process goes on just as wofully in homes of luxury and abundance. Undue immersion in business cares makes a man dull, morose, reserved, unresponsive to the gracious attentions and elevating influences of home. His thoughts never leave the ledger, the banking account, fluctuating investments, the letters of business correspondents. How can he enter into the interests of the home when forty-eight hours may find him either a Crœsus or a genteel beggar? Children must be got out of the way, for their prattle is discord and agony. And the excess of house-pride acts just as disastrously upon the temper of the wife. Neatness, system, adroit management, a fretful punctiliousness, are the ruling idols, to which everything else must be sacrificed. It is nothing if a child's sensibilities are cruelly wounded by angry words, and the hell-fire of resentment kindled in a little soul; but it is an unpardonable sin if thoughtless feet should patter across a newly-cleaned threshold, and meddlesome little hands should soil a tablecloth, or let fall some useless but elegant ornament. And so at last all the romance of early love goes, and the excess of worry cankers at the heart of those who were once sworn to mutual tenderness and fidelity. The world has stifled, if it has not killed, the higher life of sentiment and affection.

And if the fretting tyranny of care and avarice and ambition are so often fatal to the affections that rest upon the natural instincts, how much more deadly must they prove to those loftier and more subtle affections of the life which rest upon the spiritual! The more the world takes out of the deepest heart of a man in the way of thought and energy and love, the less will he have to give to God. The thorn and the wheat cannot each have the nutriment which man's nature has been prepared to give. One half of a man's faith cannot be given to God and the other half to the world, for faith is too vital to survive division after this truculent fashion. If the seed is to grow, Christ's lily, symbolising as it does a serene faith in the providence of God, must cast out the thorn. He who allows the thorn to rear itself within his heart and struggle with the seed, wastes the grace and privilege of the gospel, and receives its word of glorious opportunity in vain.

Although so much of the parable deals with the discouragements of the Galilean outlook, the work of the Sower is not in vain. Dark and depressing days were at hand; but there were many who had gained some little grasp of the principles of His teaching; the first symptoms of reaction under the stress of official opposition had left them still loyal to the truth and its obligations; and the special anxieties of the period through which they were passing, together with the opportunities for worldly preferment which were still open, had failed to thwart the growth of the chosen few in grace and in the saving knowledge of the work and person and doctrine of the Great Teacher. The Lord Jesus was not without compensations in His work. He thought of those in His own and succeeding ages who should bring forth thirty, sixty, yea, even a hundred fold, and the mortifications of the much-tried teacher and helper of men should be forgotten in the vast and enduring joy of the ingathering. Some of the later parables in the series cárry the disciples on to a stage when failure will be all but eliminated, and the great spaces of the horizon will be filled with signs of the victorious and all-prevailing kingdom.

CHAPTER X.

THE SEED AND THE MYSTERY OF ITS GROWTH.

THE Evangelist Mark inserts in his record of the discourse by the lake-shore at Capernaum, a short, picturesque, and inspiring parable which is obviously a companion to that of the Sower, and deals with some aspects of the kingdom which scarcely fall within the analogies of the introductory parable. The reaction which followed the ministry of the Baptist and the first slack in the turning tide of the Lord's own popularity, may find historic expression in the first parable, which seems to be weighted with the memory of defeat and failure. The second parable, which vindicates the Divine properties of the truth, and takes hold of those deeper facts in the heart of society which were brought into view at the ingathering of the Pentecost, was spoken to hearten Himself and His fellow-labourers, and to vindicate the faithfulness of God. Failure on man's side there may be, but wherever there is receptiveness, great spiritual changes will effect themselves, for in the seed there is a promise of power which cannot fail. The disciples need warning against impatience, self-sufficiency, unbelieving restlessness concerning the issue of their work. The pattern Sower Himself must needs sleep the sleep of death, whilst the work which He had begun is committed to that unseen providence which broods in the darkest night. But the time of ripeness draws on apace at last, and we see the Sower returning to His fields once more to gather up the gains of His early toil. And what is true upon the world-wide is true also upon the personal scale.

The first parable suggests the preparatory conditions which will affect the fruitfulness of the seed, and tacitly hints that to some extent men have these conditions under their own control. He who at first has received the truth in vain, may in due time fit himself for a more hopeful attitude to the evangel, inasmuch as his earthly life is made up of more than one sowing-time. Some hindrances to fruitfulness have been there from the beginning, and some have been artificially created or aggravated by sloth, but shrewd and honest effort may remove them. The trodden path may be ploughed up and protected against future trespassers, the underlying film of rock may be broken so as to give space downwards to the springing wheat, and thorns may be plucked up and destroyed. The sphere within which man can co-operate with God and prepare himself for the seed of the kingdom is wide and significant.

But this second parable takes us into a realm in which human power and resource are minimised. There are wonderful and unfaltering processes in the development of the seed towards which the husbandman can contribute nothing, and the working out of which he must needs await in patient faith. He can cast his handful of grain upon the ground, rake or harrow it in, and take every possible step for the protection of the field in which his seed lies buried; but his work is then practically at an end till the harvest comes, and the more thoroughly he takes the lesson home the better for the welfare of his crops. Other forces than those which his own wit and sinew contribute come into play, and quietly carry the seed through successive stages of change to its last perfection. He may guard his fields against birds, stray sheep and cattle, and may arm his household against marauding bands of Bedouin; but practically his toils are at an end for the present, and he is free to follow the common routine of his life till the thick golden ears invite the thrust of his sickle. The complex evolutions of the next few months he cannot take under his guidance, patronage, and control. He has no part in the secret changes and expansions and upbuildings which noiselessly effect themselves beneath the soil. So with the work of God by the evangel of His Son, whoever is the messenger of that evangel. Men may forsake past sin and so prepare their hearts for unknown gains when the life-giving truth comes to them. They may train themselves to give careful and undivided heed to the word preached to them through Jesus Christ. And he who has himself been transformed by the power of that word may be diligent in preaching and testifying to others. But it is impossible for us to follow step by step those wonderful changes wrought upon human souls into whose secret recesses the Spirit of God has come to brood, and to vitalise the world. We are ignorant, helpless, and so restrained by God's interdict, that we cannot enter those spheres of innermost sacredness where God Himself immediately breathes newness of life into natures once dead; but in spite of our helplessness we can calmly and confidently count on these sublime spiritual facts.

This parable, referring in the first place to

Christ's personal work and then to that of His messengers, sets forth the virtues of preaching when God inspires and confirms it. The seed cast into the earth is the published word, and what illimitable power dwells in that unpretending agency when God makes it an accepted part of His saving economies! The tendency of ecclesiasticism has always been to shift the centre of that power which quickens and purifies the soul from a word to a sacrament. But a sacrament is only the word in another form, the word with the imprint of the Lord's ordination upon it, addressing with peculiar emphasis the eye and the sense of touch as well as the sense of hearing; and what is true of the word is true of the sacrament, in no higher sense on the one hand and in no lower sense on the other. God works as wondrously through the word as through the most solemn Christian rites, and whilst we speak of the sacraments as holy mysteries, Jesus applied the same terms to the truths of the kingdom which were unfolding themselves to the apprehension of the disciples, and there is no wonder-working power present at font or altar not attending the simple declaration of the gospel. Life-giving power always sleeps in the truth, waiting only due occasion for its unfolding. The message falling from the lips of

Christ and His servants is the seed upon which these silent and noiseless forces from God's presence fasten, to change the heart of man and the spirit of mighty nations.

This parable is intended to assert the profound mystery which veils the dawn of spiritual life and the steps of its progress to maturity. The growth of the soul into the saving consciousness of God and spiritual things is distinguished from a mere manufacture, in which the part performed by man is conspicuous at every point, and the tireless whirr and rattle of the performance almost deafen the ear. The husbandman is one who modestly estimates his own wisdom and strength, and just puts himself into lowly co-operation with Nature and her amazing energies. He does little more than touch a key, which establishes some electric connexion between seed and soil, and magic factors come into play whose issues will enrich him by and by, but of whose deepest causes he can give no adequate explanation. Just where his efforts come to an abrupt end, inscrutable forces meet him, and work superbly in proportion to the sense he has of his own helplessness. The seed is a focus or rallying-point for unknown influences, which only begin to make themselves felt and seen after the tiny shower of grain has left the sower's hand.

In those obscure realms of development nestling just a little beneath the soil, God works alone, and the methods are too majestic and profound for the intermeddling of man. The sower may go his way and follow the common rounds of his appointed life, eating, drinking and holding converse with his friends by day, sleeping his full without care or disturbing dream at night; for after he has worked in the seed he can do nothing more to further its germination. No science of ancient or modern world can expedite or retard those laws of growth which hide within the husk. He has given up the seed into superhuman guardianship. Divine forces, disdaining the co-operation of man, impel the march of that which is sown towards fruitfulness, just as truly as those forces impel the silent stars.

The secret of growth is as much beyond the range of human comprehension as though it were locked away in the heart of the sun. The adept in organic chemistry knows little more about it than the rude peasant who paces the furrow or sits on the reaping machine. He may describe the physiological change which is one of the incidents of growth, and may explain how the wheat-stalk springs from a single germ-cell, and from what portion of the cell-walls the different tissues are produced. He may point out the part played by protoplasm and the part played by chlorophyll in the life of this organism. He may detect the granules of starch and of sugar, and may test successfully for the mineral salts present in the sap which fills the cells. His analysis may tell him that hydrogen, oxygen, silicon, phosphorous, iron, and many other things are present in the structure. But why the chemical reactions identified with growth should take place, and where the silent and invisible mainspring of all this movement lies, and what is the special force acting upon that mainspring, and how the sun and earth and seed have been brought into this extraordinary partnership, he cannot tell. He despairs, if he is a sensible man at least, of ever bridging the gulf between crystallisation and life. God reserves a large share in the processes of the natural year to Himself, and His operations move on in superb independence of us and our scanty knowledge. Labourer and scientist are equally incompetent for the questions which suggest themselves, and the seed has to be sown and left in the working out of its after-fortunes to an unseen providence. Man is just as helpless to lead forth all the vital properties which are hidden in the insignificant husk, as to guide Arcturus with his suns. He is left behind, like the seventy elders of Israel in

Sinai, whilst God, veiled in fire and thick darkness, lays His behests upon the spirit of nature. The biggest stride towards the golden consummation of harvest time is that which is taken when the mortal labourer has turned his back upon the fields, and is in converse with his friends or wrapped in dreamless sleep. The seed rebukes man's pride by behaving more wonderfully after it has escaped his hand, than ever it did before. "It springeth up he knoweth not how."

In spiritual as in natural things, he who is a labourer together with God must needs learn to trust and wait. With the preaching of the gospel a new act in the work of God upon the human soul begins to unfold itself, and we cannot possibly trace the subtle forces which operate in His life-giving processes. When we ask, like Nicodemus, "How can these things be?" we are pointed, by way of answer, to one of the standing mysteries of Nature. We desire to see the shining pathway of the Spirit's descent, as John saw the track of light above the head of Jesus as He stood in the waters of the Jordan, but no such spectacle is permitted, and we have to accept the fruits of joy, meekness, long-suffering, love, as the sign of the unseen presence which sanctifies. God's secret and sacred operations cannot be overwatched and supervised. The mysteries of grace resent our intrusive officiousness. The priest wants to take under his own special patronage all the subtle movements of the soul as it expands into righteousness and sanctity. Every sin must be told into his ear, and he must pronounce the absolution if it is to be effectual. He seeks to keep his finger always on the pulse of the conscience, and to gauge the ebb or flow of spiritual health. He must be always aboard the soul, like the aeronaut in his car, and open valves or throw out ballast, as the exigencies of each passing moment may indicate. He must prescribe penance or discipline and grant indulgence as seems discreet. Not content to leave God alone for a moment in His subtle work in the human soul, he must pry into its deepest recesses, and judge and counsel and dictate continually. And, at the opposite end of the ecclesiastical scale, the hot evangelist, who auctioneers men into the kingdom of heaven, and counts converts by the tap of the hammer, is under precisely the same temptation. He wants to measure, almost moment by moment, the workings of grace within the soul. The enquirer is handled with a freedom and a minuteness that may in some cases hinder rather than help. Are you sure the conviction of sin is sufficiently deep? Does the burden of its sadness press upon you till you feel it is more than you can bear? Have you that sense of the hatefulness of sin which is sure to spring up in the heart surrendered to the presence and ministrations of the Spirit? Were you conscious of some supernatural influence helping you as you made your first effort to trust in Christ Jesus the Saviour? Words of faith are put into the lips, and then almost before faith has had time to do its work the question is put, Does this act of obedient faith bring with it the assurance of God's forgiving favour? Are you now sealed with the Holy Spirit of promise? Is it a foregleam of light or a vast sunrise that has come into your nature? Now, Jesus Christ Himself did seek to test the progress of the disciples once and again with questions, "Whom say ye that I, the Son of Man, am?" but it was at rare intervals that He cross-examined them about these subtle inward secrets. Such restless and reiterated interrogations may seem to imply that the God of the gospel is on His trial, and He may not in every case chance to vindicate His covenant promise. We may project the shadows of our own lurking misgivings into other minds, and lead them to suppose that the sequence of cause and effect in the kingdom of God is not always uniform. It may be mischievous if we try to look too curiously into the soil as the seed is growing there.

Instead of harassing men with an introspective catechism that has a leaven of scepticism in it, the Christian worker must have faith in both the principles wrapped up in the seed, and in the Divine forces which prepare the soil for the seed. The work of grace is often deeply veiled. We must be satisfied with the issues, and not seek to hunt down all the latent and labyrinthine processes. Wherever the seed touches good and honest ground, there will be quickenings, verdure, fruitfulness. We must not try to supervise God and the mysteries of His grace. That work is not Divine which we can observe and verify at every step. God must be left to Himself whilst He works the greatest feat known to the history of the universe, the quickening of men to a Divine life by the word of truth.

The parable reminds us of a law of spontaneous increase which comes into play when the human conditions have been once fulfilled. "The earth bringeth forth fruit of itself." It is an attribute of the soil to be fruitful when it is dealt with by honest and reasonable methods. There are vital elements in it prearranged to meet the needs of the seed. The two things have been made for each other, and illustrate the principle of concurrent adaptation. In systems of Nature-worship the brown earth is equally honoured with the overspreading azure; for a principle of dualism is supposed to run through all things, and earth and sky are regarded as complementary sexes. When the great Teacher says that the earth bringeth forth fruit automatically,—for that is the very word He used,—He does not mean to imply that the earth could ever prove itself a fertilising power to the seed apart from the preparation it has received at the hands of its Maker; but, speaking after the manner of men, and as the outward senses judge things, the process is spontaneous, and brooks no human interposition. A virtue is present there coeval with the beginnings of organic life. The ground is pregnant with mysterious elements. Whatever the plant needs to take up through its roots has been stored there long before the footprint of man came upon the scene. The costly fertilisers the farmer may put into the soil only make good what has been recklessly taken out of it by human greed. Does the plant need mineral salts? They are there. Is iron one of its crying necessities? It is distributed through the soil in appreciable quantities. Must the corn-stalk have flint-dust to give it stiffness and rigidity? The earth is equal to the demand,

and has long stored up such resources in its treasury. Must the seed have shelter from the extremes of heat and cold? The earth, like a kind foster-mother, tempers the severity of the one and the wasting fervour of the other. When the soil has once received its trust at the hands of man, it asks no more, for it has long learned its lesson and is quite competent to undertake the rest.

The worker must expect, having sown the seed, to find an instinctive responsiveness to its requirements in the hearts of men. There are brooding influences in the heart which correspond to the potentialities of the seed,—influences which have been instilling themselves there from the very beginning, and are ever instilling themselves anew. When the heart is broken and the will surrendered to the rule of God's will, forces and affections appear in the man which league themselves with the great forces of the deathless seed and work wonders, introduced there, of course, by the Divine Spirit; for this parable postulates and broadly prophesies the mission of the Spirit in the regeneration of mankind. The conditions which make the human heart inhospitable to the seed lie near the surface, are often artificial, and in many cases will prove only temporary. As labourers in God's service, we have to trust the secret energies which are dealing with human nature, and which go on in complete independence of our ever varying moods. It is not for us to overlook all the subtle developments of mind and heart and conscience, as the man sometimes itches to do who thinks that one called to office in the church must needs be a busybody. The human heart, which is not without light and inward leading, may resent being over-tutored and over-superintended from without in its most sacred movements and functions. Men are sometimes teased into antagonism to religion and distaste for its holy principles and institutions. Religion, as illustrated by some misguided souls, seems to mean petty interference and dictation, a fretting tyranny of the leading-strings which no great nature can possibly brook. When the right word has been spoken, and the right truth clearly and effectually set forth, let it have time. We are required to have faith in the permanent moral and spiritual properties God has put, and is still putting, into human life, and that faith may sometimes be tried for long. The fiat which creates the seed prepares the soil. The gospel must never be thought of as a foreign element introduced into human hearts, and needing to be attended every moment by an interpreter and a go-between. There is a mutual affinity and understanding between the seed and the soil, and the speech of the gospel cannot, in the long-run, be an unknown tongue to any being God Almighty has made. Meddlesome officialism, an anxiety begotten of our own sense of self-importance which makes us restless and intrusive, a tendency to search other hearts rather than our own, a distrustfulness about the issue scarcely separable from unbelief, may thwart the fertility of the soil.

In the growth of the seed there is a predetermined order of development no art of man can invert or disarrange. "First the blade, then the ear, and then the full corn in the ear." Each is comely and needful, and the succeeding stages are an earnest of the consummation. It would be a poor ear that grew without blade or stalk to support and lift it into the sun, and such an ear could have no prospect of maturity. And the analogy holds when the gospel becomes fruitful in the life of either the individual or the nation. Measured steps of progression are inevitable, the step from the buried seed to early promise, the step from early promise to approaching maturity, and the step from approaching maturity to full and lavish fruition. And all such steps take time. There is no necessary guilt or sinfulness in immaturity. The cultivator of the soil, as he looks out over fields upon which a faint tinge of green is dawning, does not frown because the blade precedes the bending ear. There is a perfection of blade as well as of ear and ripened grain, and through these succeeding stages there may be a gracious freedom from the blights of wilful disobedience. Precisely the same qualities are not to be expected or required in the early as in the later religious life; and if vital activities are in progress, we must trust God for the rest.

The grace, insight, and capability of the apostles themselves were produced by methods that were more or less slow and tedious. At the time these parables were first uttered, John could not have written his own First Epistle; and it is a question whether he would have shown any appreciation of it if it had been written by some one else. Not one in the Twelve would have accepted the theology afterwards enunciated in the Epistle to the Romans. That was a fruit of more mature thought and experience than belonged to them at this early stage. If the Master had proposed to send the morbid and forebodeful Thomas on a mission to Rome, the cry that Jesus was beside Himself would have been heard in the inner circle of the faithful. But Thomas at last went further afield than that. The mighty labours and sacrifices of the after-times were impossible as yet. Faith, spiritual insight, fitness for service, had to be evolved and built up step by step through the reciprocal action of grace and discipline in the coming days. The form and order of spiritual growth has been determined by the Author and Giver of life.

This inflexible order asserted in the parable is sometimes forgotten. We expect the sobriety and chastened temper of age from those who are feeling the first thrill of spiritual life. The children of the kingdom are expected to be as grave as Paul the aged, or Mnason the believing patriarch. The lightnesses of youth are eyed with as much suspicion as though they were vices. The burden of a formulated system of theology must be grafted on to the tender upspringing instincts of infancy, and a young man must accept the theology of the church councils first and be a Christian afterwards. That is putting the ear before the blade. In God's order there must be an inward sense of spiritual things before there can be a defined science of Divine truth. The graces of young Christians, like their theologies, differ from those of older Christians, and we must not disparage the one at the expense of the other. The transition periods required in the development of the later and more symmetrical mental and spiritual excellencies must never be left out of our reckoning. The process of building up in faith and virtue depends to some extent upon the reaction of the personal history upon the mind and character of the man who has subjected himself to the will of Christ.

The sowing and the reaping days must be full of strenuous and unresting toil. But, alternating with these, there are days on which we feel our helplessness, and must leave the work already done to God's care. Our life will mainly be made up of routine and quiet waiting. And this temper of tranquillity illustrated by the sower, who puts his head on a thornless pillow and sleeps without a care, is a befitting characteristic of Christ's servants and fellow-labourers. It is sometimes said, if religious men believed what they assert about the evil and peril of sin, life would become an agonised insomnia. To sit down to a pleasant meal would be cold-blooded callousness, and to laugh at the humours of the world in which we live, treason. That would be perfectly true if we were toiling in a world bereft of its God, and in which no ministering Spirit from above took charge of our work when our part was done. Jesus Christ felt the enigmas of sin, and yearned, O how pitifully! over human souls. Yet His life and temper were placid. For thirty years He did not venture into public religious movements, and even when His time of official service had come, He followed the routine of an average Jew, attending feasts, lending Himself to the claims of friendship, making Himself sociable even with well-disposed Pharisees, sleeping, when worn with toil, and perhaps dreaming of His Father's heaven. His rule of life seems to be reflected in this picture of the sower sleeping after he had cast in his seed, and then quietly passing to other duties. And at last He withdrew from visible participation in the affairs of men, and carried on His work by unseen ministries in unseen worlds. From the fields where He had scattered seed He went back to His home, leaving the truth to germinate more wondrously than whilst He was present amongst men in the flesh. He knew there were processes which could not be hurried, and He was content to commit His seed to those faithful and measureless spiritual influences which were already brooding in the hearts of men, and which, under the ministry of the coming Spirit, were to produce such wonderful fruit.

The parable intimates that when the world is ready for the great consummation, He who has left His fields will come back again. He is looking out for the ripeness of the race in truth, righteousness, and love, and when the signs appear there will be no delay. He will "straightway" thrust in His sickle, and His fellow-workers will attend by His side to share the harvest joy. Excluded from all part in the deepest mysteries of growth, they shall yet share in the feasting and the song. They are suffered to appear once more upon the scene when it is best of all to be there.

CHAPTER XI.

CHRIST'S VIEW OF THE SCRIPTURES

THE imitation of Christ must include His temper of mind towards the Scriptures, for if we depart from His view-point upon this difficult subject we can scarcely claim to call ourselves by His name. To sympathise with His appreciations of the law and the prophets, and to determine, if possible, the precise import of those appreciations, becomes a matter of vital importance to us if we are to think and act and pray in harmony with His pattern. This collection of books had been of supreme interest to Him from His boyhood, for it was upon the lips of the men whose special vocation it was to interpret them, that He had hung at His memorable visit to the Temple, and had asked questions the suggestiveness of which filled the bystanders with amazement. It was the voice of the Scriptures, read in the synagogues every Sabbath day, which always drew Him thither in whatever town He might be sojourning. His reverence for these documents was shown by the fact that, according to Jewish custom, He stood up to read in the synagogue. This was no blind and servile conformity to an established code of manners, for our Lord was a hater of shams, vain shows, and unrealities, and when a rite was empty, barren, or misleading, He showed no hesitation whatever in setting it aside. Alas! for the disciple who pays less honour to the sacred books than the Great Teacher Himself. He rarely availed Himself of those special sources of knowledge which were open to Him as the Divine Son, and thought of His work, office, and appointed sufferings in the light of the Scriptures, accounting Himself more constantly beholden to the guidance and encouragement made ready there, than even those who are human and nothing more. And yet at the same time He was neither a slave to mechanical theories of inspiration nor a blind idolater of parchments. He went back to the first principles behind the detail of Mosaic legislation, and claimed right and liberty to set forth those principles in new forms and higher applications than they had received from the first lawgivers and rulers of God's people. The method was in sharp opposition to that pursued by scribes and Pharisees, who worshipped external forms and crystallised the momentary phase of a living truth.

The training and providential surroundings of the Great Teacher prepared Him to view the Old Testament records with a reverent breadth. In all probability He did not Himself possess a copy of the book of which He was the hero. He read and heard it in the uncorrupted tongue in which it was originally written. He also listened to the popular paraphrases of the scribes, as they presented it in the speech of the hour. Amongst the Greek - speaking populations the Septuagint translation was used, and He Himself quoted from it. To put undue emphasis upon the verbal form of a book is not the temptation of one who is accustomed to its use in different tongues. Under such conditions He would come to think much of the substance and little of the drapery of the message. Where the mere letter of a book commands undue homage, translations are rigorously proscribed. The Parsee, the Confucianist, the Brahman once looked upon it as an act of sacrilege to translate his sacred records into foreign tongues. The Jews had left that view of things far behind, in spite of their narrowness and religious bigotry, and the only survival of it was to be found in those scholarly castes which assumed that the law must be known in the very phrases of its original proclamation, and of such castes our Lord was the sworn foe. Apart from what was taught Him by His own broad and holy instincts, the meagreness of the academic training received by Jesus Christ would lead Him to think more of the unchanging and incorruptible substance of the message rather than of its precarious and uncertain letter. All language is imperfect, for it is coloured by the mental and moral shortcomings of those who have been accustomed to use it; but God may speak irreducible realities through it nevertheless. He who has that spiritual sensibility which recognises the Divine forces pulsating in a revelation, will not be repelled by the inevitable crudeness in the mere accident of its form.

Our Lord did not treat the Scriptures from the standpoint of the letter, but from that of the spirit. In the Sermon on the Mount, which is an instructive illustration of His attitude upon this subject, He went back to the first essentials, and in doing so claimed that He was preparing for the larger fulfilment of both the law and the prophets. He recognised that the decalogue itself was meant to cover the realm of thought and emotion as well as of outward conduct, and made the prohibition of murder to forbid those angry passions which are the unseen starting-points of the coarsest forms of the crime. Early precepts, which had been narrowed in condescension to human dullness and infirmity, must needs be expanded into larger and more comprehensive rules of life. In one case it seems as though He were not broadening out the principle enforced by Moses, but condemning and abrogating it. The code of a carefully-meted, retaliatory justice must give place in His kingdom to mercy. But in all that He was teaching on the lines taken up by Moses, and was not at cross purposes with him, inasmuch as " an eye for an eye and a tooth for a tooth " was the judicial axiom introduced for a time to check the unbridled licence of revenge; and mercy, after all, is a larger form of justice. The Sabbath law He saw to be a law of love, and set aside conventional applications of it in which the original motive had been obscured, and left man-made byelaws to take care of themselves. He repealed a ritual which had once been divinely ordained, and felt Himself free from the reproach of revolutionary innovation, because He was at the same time demonstrating in better ways the ethical reality of which the rite had been a shadow. He treated the old Testament Scriptures as a book of beginnings,—Divine beginnings, it is true,—

but beginnings which it was His special work to consummate. In dealing with this mass of venerated literature, He must needs take hold of the broad ultimate principles contained therein, and not assume that the application of those principles can always be measured in feet and inches. Under the concrete example He finds the changeless and eternal law. Jesus saw in the Books of Moses, and the Psalms and the Prophets, more than a fabric of godly tradition, for He put the holy commandments in contrast to the injunctions of men, and charged the devotees of tradition with trespass against the high living authority of God Himself.

Jesus went further still, and recognised the fact that the Old Testament revelations were adjusted to the defective moral states of those addressed therein, and that God's message can only reach its ethical fulness and perfection when it shapes itself to the needs of a more highly-disciplined and regenerated people. He frankly admits limitations in the earlier disclosures of God's mind, thus bringing Himself into conflict with those who had lost the sense of religious progress and were ever turning their faces to the past. " For your hardness of heart Moses wrote you this commandment." The ideal law of creation allowed no place for divorce, and in making this concession Moses was putting marriage upon a less holy and Divine level than at the beginning. It was the only thing for the moment that he could do; but our Lord's reference shows that He at least did not regard the earlier legislation, though divinely authorised, as perfect and final. It was attempered, in its successive acts and stages, to the varying capacities of the race in contrasted periods of its training; and in weighing the questions at the root of a doctrine of inspiration, we have to picture to ourselves, not only the kind of disclosure of Himself and His will the Eternal can make, but no less the kind of disclosure the people can receive. The maxim is true of secular as of inspired legislation, that it cannot proceed very far in advance of the times. The books of the earlier portions of the Bible must be judged in the light of that truism. Those who deny that the Scripture is a revelation from God, inasmuch as it contains some things which seem crude, tentative, imperfect, frequently do so on the ground that God might have given faultless disclosures of Himself and His will by strictly intellectual methods, and that it is incredible He should identify Himself with documents which have the least suspicion of looseness or inaccuracy in any of their contents. But the moral is the only pathway by which man can arrive at knowledge of the Divine, and a revelation is compelled to bend itself at some points to the condition of those who are to receive it, and that which is not quite ideal from some standpoints may be practically the most perfect. The less will prepare the way for the larger revelation, and he who catches the true moral keynote in the teachings of Moses will be prepared to listen to the Prophet of whom he spake. That was a principle our Lord consistently asserted. "Ye have not His word abiding in you, for whom He sent, him ye believe not."

The Great Teacher contemplated the sacred records of the past from the practical standpoint, and found there the active germ-forces of all saving religion, and this aspect of the subject absorbed Him. He displayed no interest in the matters at which Holy Scripture began to touch the frontiers of science, literature, history, psychology. If He had adopted any other course, it would have tended to minimise the solitary significance of His one idea. When He declared that the Holy Ghost spake by David, it would have satisfied curiosity, and have helped the human mind to a theory of inspiration if He had said where the human ended and the Divine began, and how much of David and

David's temperament and training were left in the process. By Him all things were made, but He said nothing about the mere ways and means by which an Almighty fiat built the universe. He claimed to be before Abraham, but never touched a question of Old Testament criticism, or separated the Pentateuch into its constituent parts. He did not set Himself up as a court of appeal on the records of Israelitish history, although He might have saved the present century much time and thought if He had entered upon that inviting field. On all such questions He accepted and assumed the traditions current amongst the Jews, and, in so far as those traditions were vital to His own work and authority, put the stamp of His august endorsement upon them. Why did He keep His own supernatural knowledge in abeyance when He might have corrected possible errors, and have obviated the academic strifes of His later disciples? Such subjects were side-issues, and did not enter into the main current of the movement He was to set in action. He gave Himself to the duty of the hour, and His mission and message were of such overwhelming significance that much of the supernatural knowledge in the background of His personality did not pass into His working consciousness. The principle given to His heralds, "Salute no man by the way," was one of the guiding precepts of His own vocation. He had not time or strength to parley with science, pass the time of day with scholarship, or enter into debate with the scribes who were filling up the span of human life with antiquarian persiflage. It was not for Him to sift out the primitive traditions used by the sacred writers, to separate parable from literal history, and folk-lore from the religious truth it had been made to enshrine. It was enough that the breath of the Eternal was in the book, and He came to it as the humblest and most reverent of us, although, of course, with a larger interest in its intimations.

The Scriptures were designed to awaken in men a sense of God, and of the possibilities of His power not to be acquired elsewhere. Through their perusal the lowly and the docile will be made to feel the thrill of the Divine presence, and catch the imperative voice of the Most High as on a fire-girt Sinai. In the controversy which followed the Bethesda miracle, Jesus upbraided the Jews because they had "neither heard the voice of His Father, nor seen His form," inasmuch as "they had not His word abiding in them." He was not speaking at that particular moment of God's inaccessibility to the methods of physical demonstration, but of the study of the Scriptures.

The Old Testament word was so able to enter into men as to bring true reflections of the Divine personality into their thought and true messages of the Divine voice into their conscience, and to all such experience these Jews were strangers. If men approach these records aright, God will ever use them as the path by which He will draw near, making men conscious of His majesty and sensible of His will. He who has seen the ever-living theophanies with which the Old Testament trembles, will carry the glory in his heart, and recognise an unfolding of the power and word of the Eternal in the Son of Man. And in the controversy upon the subject of the resurrection, Matthew's gospel makes Jesus present practically the same view of these ancient writings. "Ye do err, not knowing the scriptures, nor the power of God." The two clauses are practically synonymous, and he who feels the true force of the Old Testament teaching will have such a sense of God's infinite strength and resource, that the problem of the resurrection—be it a complication arising out of the customs of Levirate marriage or anything else—will be no longer a stumbling-block. The sacred writings of the Jews were a record of successive acts of power for the vindication of the covenant, and of the fidelity with which God sought through long centuries to bring near the blessings of the covenant; and he who reads the record aright will always feel the nearness, sufficiency, and strength of the Eternal Presence that asserts itself there. The books tremble with the infinite, like a temple to which God and His flame-winged seraphs have come, but, alas! some lack eyes for the vision. Men must learn through the word their lessons of Divine power, and if they neglect or despise it, must continue in fatal ignorance to the end.

In the gospel according to St Luke, which was not compiled under the influence of Jewish ideas, and which handled Jewish prejudices with not a little freedom, we find that Jesus is made to declare the sufficiency of the Scriptures for all the ends of persuasion and faith. Whatever limitations of outward form they may have, nothing is found there to weaken or discredit the soul-saving validity of their message. "They have Moses and the prophets, let them hear them." Supernatural sanctions operate there at least quite as forcible as one would bring with him if he were sent from the realms of the dead. The writings will convince as many as wish to put themselves in the way of being convinced, and it is not a part of God's order for the government of mankind to force conviction on the unwilling. For all moral and religious ends, these books stand on one and the same level with the authority of a direct and immediate herald from the realms of the unseen. The ancient message has enough in it to keep men from selfishness here and the penalty of selfishness hereafter, and Dives would never have been so inconsiderate and luxurious if he had listened with more faith and reverence to the word read in the synagogue every Sabbath day. By the writings of Moses and the prophets, the standard of an equitable responsibility is maintained amongst men, and that could not be so if the documents lacked Divine authority. He who is offended by the rude and archaic cast of thought and phraseology in the letter of the Scriptures, is more sensitive on the intellectual than on the moral side of his nature; and the very marks of humanness on the revelation may give it higher efficency as a test of character and a means for the fulfilment of religious ends. There may sometimes be a luxurious mental fastidiousness as hurtful and as perilous as the passion for splendour and gluttony in Dives, and the moral nature can only be raised to a normal level of activity by mortifying that which has outgrown and overshadowed it.

Jesus affirms the inviolability of all the principles underlying what might seem subsidiary elements in the Old Testament records. "The scripture cannot be broken." The assertion is solemn, and more or less startling, for our Lord is arguing from a minor detail in justification of His use of the title, "Son of God." When the Bible concedes an official name to those whom God invests with His power and informs with His truth, a mysterious and many-sided fact is suggested, and the word admits of no retraction. A riddle is put before us we may do well to ponder, and God is not so solitary as we may assume, for the Psalmists were not men given to vain and frivolous speech. To every part of Scripture there belong attributes and prerogatives which make it unchangeable. Nothing they contain shall be set at nought. The Son's birthright of honour, power, dominion, is sufficiently secured by the covenant of the Scriptures; and even if shortcoming is proved against the mere handwriting of the charter which secured His crown-rights, the charter itself could not be thrust aside. The Divine word already uttered was more abiding than the hills of the earth or the stars of the sky. Jesus once spoke of Himself as greater than the Temple, because the vision of its coming desolation, its roofless shrines, its forsaken courts, its desecrated altars, was already before Him, but He never spake of Himself as greater than the word, because that was His own witness, and was to endure to all ages, speaking in unchanging accents and pulsating with the life of the Eternal.

In the view of Jesus, the Scriptures contained the clews by which all candid and earnest seekers might find the appointed Giver of eternal life. He had found there correspondences with His own Messianic consciousness not a few, and He set Himself to honour the preintimations of the prophets, alike in matters that were vital and matters that seemed without commanding significance. He gives no sanction to some of the extravagant phantasies with which the history of interpretation has made us familiar, but He does affirm that the set of this wonderful past of which the sacred writings are landmarks, has been towards Himself, and that meek and lowly souls may find the clearest foreshadowings of His work and person in these special documents. The books read in the synagogues could not fail to put our Lord's contemporaries in the pathway of Divine leading, and prepare the way of faith for every sincere and open mind. If they would take the first step, and become humble learners in the schools of the lawgiver and the prophets, the second step would be inevitable, and they should yet believe in Him of whom Moses and the prophets spake.

It was not as a court of appeal in controversy only that the Lord used the Scriptures. The missionary to the cultivated races of Asia sometimes quotes the Sacred Books of the East to make good the positions he teaches, but those books, however interesting as literature, do not feed the springs of his personal life. The Old Testament Scriptures had just as important and as assured a place in our Lord's inner thought as in His public teaching. He used its maxims for the lighting up of His own pathway, and the defence of His own faith in the hour of darkness and temptation. His personal forecasts of suffering and death were confirmed by the inspired word. Its utterances were red beacon lights, showing the pathway to the cross. As He hung prostrate beneath the burden of His redeeming passion, it was only in the holy speech of Scripture that He ventured to bewail His own desolation of soul, and at last speak of His emergent faith. He did not discredit past revelations by falling back upon His own superhuman resources of wisdom and knowledge. He had been baptized and commended to the people of Israel by the witness of John; the voice attesting His Sonship, and declaring the good pleasure of the Father, had already spoken from the open heavens. His communion with the Father had been immediate and unbroken. From the days of His boyhood onwards He had a consciousness of more intimate mysterious relationship with the Most High than that possessed by the most conspicuous saints; but He did not trust only to the voice from above, or the voice whispering within. The word must interact upon and co-operate with His consciousness as He read it in the synagogue at Nazareth. The prophet declares that the Spirit had anointed Him to open prison doors, and heal human sickness, and proclaim the acceptable year of the Lord. And then His own voice follows that of the prophet, "This day is the scripture fulfilled in your ears." A new sense of accomplishment had come to Him,—come, too, on a day of riot, hostility, persecution, which was only too sure a presage of the end. He was already beginning to feel that the prison doors must be opened from the inside, and that He Himself must pass into the prison-house; that He could only heal men by bearing their sickness and carrying their infirmity; and that He must pay the great ransom price Himself, as He proclaimed and brought near the acceptable year of the Lord. His forecasts of personal suffering are confirmed by the word. In its mirror He saw the visage of a Messiah marred beyond that of the sons of men. He tried to get the disciples to look at His death in the light of these solemn necessities announced in the Scriptures. It was the declaration of the Father's will concerning Him in the Scriptures which helped Him to maintain the sweetness of His resignation, and inspired Him for His cross and passion. He looked there for direction, encouragement, strength, and treated the written word as though it were the guardian and companion spirit of His personal consciousness. If the letter had its trivial blemishes, His sympathy with the essential substance was so complete that the blemish was forgotten. Christ recognised the limitations of past revelations, and treated them with an intelligent freedom and breadth; but nothing He saw in them detracted from the heedfulness with which He studied their intimations, and the loyalty with which He responded to their most exacting calls. Men can never be true imitators of Christ unless they pay equal honour to the book which was at once His court of appeal when addressing others, and a spring of light and strength and filial obedience in His personal life. Neglect of the Bible, or flippancy of tone in dealing with it, is an omen of religious degeneracy and degradation sad as that which overtook the Jews who were Christ's contemporaries.

CHAPTER XII.

LEGAL AND EVANGELICAL GREATNESS.

IT was both unfitting and impossible that Jesus Christ should directly teach the perfect system of faith which ultimately centred in His work and person. It was no more a part of His mission to preach Himself than it was a part of the Baptist's. This explains the gaps, omissions, silences which thrust themselves upon our attention when we compare the teaching of Jesus with the theology of Paul. And yet in the course of His public ministry He prepared a place for those evangelical conceptions which were hereafter to be formulated, defined, and identified in their deepest and most essential potencies with His own sacrificial death. His reiterated praises of child-likeness and its significant relation to the kingdom; His assertion that poverty of spirit is a condition of enrichment; the emphasis He places upon humility; the condemnation of the doctrine of human merit in the parable of the servants, who, having toiled in the field by day, must minister in the home by night, and then declare that they are but unprofitable servants, contrasted, too, with the other parable, in which the lord is spoken of as girding himself to minister to his own servants; and especially the startling statement after the Baptist has been praised in terms of all but matchless honour, that the least in the kingdom of heaven is greater than he,—imply and postulate a doctrine of grace one and the same with that taught in the Epistle to the Romans, and almost compelling the conclusion that justification must be by faith in the holy, unselfish sacrifice of another.

John the Baptist represents the sum of what discipline and training can do for the human mind and character. It is a misfortune for his reputation that his lot should have been cast in such close proximity to Jesus Christ, the ideal man of the new era that was emerging. Just as the planet next the sun is but rarely seen, and because of the sea of intense light in which it is set, we have an inadequate conception of its splendour, so the lofty excellence of the man into whom all the best forces of the old dispensation were gathered, is all but lost in the transcendent spiritual splendour of the great Son of God. No personal disciple or follower of Jesus Christ could be brought into comparison with him for a moment. His character was marked by a strength, a lowliness, a sustained fidelity, a uniform self-consistency, lacking in the kings, prophets, and righteous men of olden time. Illustrious and significantly expressive are those traits of character that have been preserved for us as by instantaneous photography, a stability that the frowns of kings could not move, a self-abnegation that the luxuries of palaces could not corrupt, an unworldliness that no pomp could overawe and no desert-rigour fret, a fidelity that neither imprisonment nor death could unsettle or disturb, a touching humility that for eighteen centuries has been a living rebuke to the vain-glorious tempers of nominal Christians.

Nature and the supernatural may each have contributed factors to this impressive personality. Like Isaac, John was the child of old age, and that may have left him free from some of the more violent temptations of the flesh, and neither wine nor strong drink had ever inflamed his blood. But the child of old age often lacks force, vehemence, reformative enthusiasm, as is seen in the case of Isaac. If such a constitutional defect existed in the Baptist, it was compensated by special inspiration; for he was "filled with the Holy Ghost from his mother's womb," and was never without a sense of the high vocation he had received. And the scrupulous and untiring self-discipline to which he gave himself was worthy of the inspiration he received, and the mission he accomplished worthy of his birth, inspiration, and self-discipline combined.

This character of consummate strength and fidelity compelled the reverence of the ruthless despot and sensualist Herod, for we are told that he accounted John righteous and holy. Coarse, impassive crowds, stiffened with knots of supercilious priests and scribes, were moved to profound moral excitement by the wonder of his devout and zealous life, and the prophetic anticipations which fell from his lips. The word of the angel was fulfilled, and he was great in the presence of the Most High. He had the distinction which belongs to a prince of the council chamber. What higher honour could be given to a saint of the old dispensation than that of baptizing the Messiah, and commending Him to the faith and loyalty of the people He was commissioned to rule? The Baptist's character was its own attestation. He did no miracle. Had sign and wonder been wrought by the saintly hermit, it might have tempted the crowds to a new idolatry.

The appointed Judge of men, the Son of Man Himself, declares that this heroic herald had hitherto been quite unmatched in spirit, office, mission.

But this lofty and judicial eulogium is followed by an incredible qualification. In all that constitutes true greatness, the meanest recipient of the gospel surpasses the most loyal and devoted servant of the Law. Legal and evangelical excellence are brought into comparison with each other, and the most glorious example of the one is pronounced inferior to the most elementary embodiment of the other. Christian mediocrity outshines Jewish distinction, and the mere dwarf of the new dispensation prevails against the giant of the old.

We are startled at the paradox, and half tempted to resent the strange judgement it implies. It is as though the laurel were plucked from the brow of one who had justly earned it, and bestowed upon some frail camp-follower of the Prophet of Nazareth. The least might chance to be the woman who was a sinner against the sacred ethic of family life, a cold-blooded and brazen tax-gatherer for the conquering pagan, a dying bandit or highwayman, a missionary who was turned back from his vocation by peril and hardship, an ill-taught, lisping child. We are under the spell of hero-worship, and are jealous for this high-minded and unswerving prince of heroes, who is praised in one breath and underrated in the next. Conduct is the supreme thing, and men who are conspicuous for their integrity and disinterestedness must be honoured, or we shall find ourselves falling into the Antinomianism which makes much of faith and little of obedience to the law. Hero-worship, however, is an insidious form of idolatry, and its spirit may keep us from doing justice to the greatest of all heroes, who gave Himself for us, and who reflects the only enduring greatness upon human nature it can possibly possess.

Did Jesus Christ mean by these words greatness of status or greatness of character? Both: for they are inseparable in His teaching, although the status is bestowed by the free act of grace before the character which corresponds to it is perfectly achieved.

The life that is based on the grace which is the foundation-principle of the new kingdom, touches altitudes of grandeur unreached by the life that rests upon mere legalism. The crucial distinction between the Jew and the disciple of Jesus Christ is this, that the one works out in order that he may receive his crown of recompense, whilst the other is crowned and enriched and endowed at the very beginning by the free mercy of God, so that he may work out the appointed duties of his life. The best men of the old dispensation had only glimpses of the great principles of this latter-day privilege. The Baptist had his rigid legal limitations,—limitations which his unbending scrupulosity forbade him to overpass. The link of sympathy between the Baptist's disciples and the better sections of the Pharisees is a sufficient indication of his legal standing-ground. The task John was attempting in the desert was that of working out his own salvation and that of his generation. Gleams of evangelical hope had visited him now and again, and yet the gleams were but faint and fitful. In a strange outburst of inspired discernment he had spoken of the young Prophet of Nazareth as the Lamb of God who should take away the sin of the world. The testimony was addressed to his own most thoughtful and mature disciples, whose past profiting might well bring them within the range of that sacrificial virtue. To publicans, soldiers, Jewish tradesmen, he had no such gospel. For the time being at least, and for years to come, the only message which seemed to fit them was, "Do," "Be content," "Avoid exactions," "Be pitiful." Simon and Andrew, James and John, might hear of expiation and forgiveness, but the comfort and healing of these higher truths could scarcely come at once to the conscience-smitten rabble. John was bound by the stern genius of his own training. Legal axioms exerted a restraining influence upon his own sense of privilege. If he had been permitted to know and teach a fuller and a freer gospel, he might have been spared some of those dark mental dubitations which came to him in his imprisonment. God for him was the Judge who weighed human actions, rather than the Benefactor whose recompense anticipated service; and whatever boldness he might have before his fellows, he could have no boldness before God till he had met Him as a Judge.

And herein lies the clew to the amazing gospel paradox uttered by Jesus Christ. To the man who discerns the freeness and universality of Divine grace, God can give more than the best, the strongest, the most faithful can deserve. The Divine bounty that waits to lavish itself upon the believer in Jesus Christ is infinite, and eclipses those meagre possibilities which are inherent in the best forms of finite righteousness and service. He is greatest who best glorifies God, and God is more glorified by what men take at His hands than by the most strenuous ministries they render to His cause. Christ's past as well as His future greatness was that of a recipient, and the Father was ever bestowing anew that of which He had emptied Himself. It was the Son's chief distinction that He saw how the Divine Fatherhood was an eternal giving, and all brought into His kingdom should have the same blessed insight.

That doctrine of grace upon which the new kingdom was founded brought with it all but incredible privilege. The disciple united to his Saviour and King would no longer need to wander tremulously through the deserts listening for the awful voice of the Most High, and bowing down in terror like Moses or Elijah before the unveiling of His majesty. He would no longer worship the Holy One of Israel from afar with trembling awe, but would be brought nigh, and have boldness of access through faith. He would have the right of a son, and a son is higher than the highest prophet, and would share the mystic nature of God just as truly as a human son shares the blood of his fathers. And in the possession of such a seed, he would have a higher earnest of personal sanctity and righteousness than could possibly come to the man who was most scrupulously setting himself to keep the law. He would have a sense of the acceptableness of his work to God wanting in the loftiest reformers of the past; for he who does a little act in the spirit of love, which is the note of the new kingdom, would find a smile of approval resting upon it wanting to the most heroic achievements of the past, which were necessarily based upon motives of duty and righteousness rather than upon the more perfect motive of love. In the new kingdom of God a power would be received which would make the meanest truer benefactors of their race than those who acted most valiantly under the inferior help and inspiration of the past.

The man who stood within the kingdom had exercised in the act of entering it a humility profounder than that of the Baptist. The preacher of the wilderness was conspicuous for his humility, and a contrast to those current types of piety which were full of supercilious assumption. His asceticism was adopted as a sign that he did not think himself worthy of those providential bounties which others accepted as their common right and with little due sense of gratitude. Perhaps in his own life of self-mortification he intended to represent the unworthiness and backsliding of the nation to which he belonged. In those degenerate days, many a man, stained with every delinquency, regarded himself as a saint by a process of ethnic and ritual imputation. John's rigours of life were an impressive protest against all such notions. He declared himself, and the nation of which he formed a part, to be alike unworthy, and fit objects for the Divine displeasure. In his relation to Jesus he also displays most tender and pathetic humility. He had received an unmistakable vocation from heaven, but knew that his kinsman had received a yet more wonderful vocation. He felt himself not worthy to be the slave of Jesus Christ, or to do the meanest task in His service. His meekness was such that he was incapable of the least twinge of jealousy when he saw Christ's growing popularity, and felt that his own day was gone. Yet he feels that they belong to the same realm, that there was some kind of footing for relationship between the two, similar perhaps to that of the king and his favoured slave. But behind the faith of the new kingdom there is a yet deeper humility, for it is more difficult to bow oneself to be saved by the pain and ignominy of another, than to be the attendant of an august sovereign. Such an one has to put himself into a different category, for he has to confess that the felon's cell is his place and final condemnation his right, and to accept free pardon from one who redeems him. He has to enter the kingdom by an act of gracious enfranchisement to which the self-respecting Jew as a rule could not stoop. He must be brought to see that there is no difference between his own demerit and that of the basest Gentile offender against virtue and righteousness, and that was no easy task, for even the Jewish bandit had the religious pride of his race. Humbling himself to receive Christ as his righteousness, he becomes greater through lowliness than a prophet or even the Lord's forerunner. The man who dreams that it is easy to be humble and accept salvation as a gift, does not yet know himself, for such lowliness is the highest feat of self-conquest.

This paradox of grace may be interpreted by the difference between hope and faith, for the one is the note of the Old and the other of the New Covenant. The two words may almost touch, and indeed are sometimes interchangeably translated in the Authorised Version, but the lines of thought they mark diverge into immense separations. Jesus did not underestimate or disparage Old Testament privilege. The earlier saints were visited with inspiring forecasts of the long-expected light and gladness. The Baptist had a passing flash of insight into the mystery of Christ's sacrifice, but the vision never revisited him in its original clearness.

Like a mountain peak faintly looming through the sunrise and then passing away, the apocalypse died out and a strange eclipse came over the spirit of his latter days. Hope was centred on One who was to come, but the hope was imperfectly defined. It prepared for the salvation of God rather than made it a present benediction. When the astronomer measures the angle of light formed by the rays of two stars on his theodolite, and works out therefrom the distance of some far-off star, the slightest inaccuracy in measuring the angle will represent a difference of millions of miles in his calculations. And so the widest distinctions of life, privilege, and destiny take their rise in the fine demarcation between hope and faith.

The faith of the kingdom implies a more perfect participation in the joy of God than was possible to those who were shut up within the law. The self-mortification and fasting which marked John's career implied a lack,—a lack which kept him back for a time from the highest distinction of his destiny. Jesus Christ, in reply to a question concerning fasting, intimated that there could be no sad asceticism for those who were sharing the Bridegroom's joy and dwelling in the light of His presence. Profound and persistent sadness, however heroic the qualities with which it may be associated, is a detraction from true greatness of life and character. It was Paul's joyfulness on the way to Rome which made him the true sovereign of the rest, who cringed like slaves before the fury of the storm. Men respond to pure joyfulness as to the day-dawn, and he who lacks it cannot be regarded as one who has touched the true goal of being. The rejoicing spirits belong to the highest circles of spiritual fellowship, and God delights to dwell with them.

He who is in the kingdom has learned the deeper secret of sanctity, and by the gift of grace can rise higher than the Baptist through his assiduous life of fasting, meditation, and prayer. The child, with all the resources of civilisation at his beck, is greater than Alexander the Great,— great through the gifts of an illustrious line of inventors rather than by his own force and skill. And under that sense of soul-purifying love, which is a free inspiration within the believer, loftier excellencies of character can be achieved than by John, who was living under the stern constraint of righteousness; for the least act done in love outweighs in God's sight the most heroic things done by those who, however high their motives, lack this Divine impulse. In the sanctity which comes through the mystical union of the believer with the God of love, there is a promise and a power of expansion wanting in the finest types of righteousness which were produced by the law. After a month's growth, a tulip may look a much more imposing thing than an acorn, but the succeeding years will tell a different tale. Although the character represented by John the Baptist may have seemed for the time being much nobler than that represented by John the Apostle, yet we know full well that the latter reached, through his participation in the life and spirit of his Master, a loftier perfection of temper and of service. No advance was possible to the Baptist till some great expansion of his outlook had come and a new set of motives had germinated in his life. In all purely moral heroism there is a limit beyond which it is impossible to pass, and the forerunner had reached that limit. Indeed, he seems to show in the end symptoms of deterioration and decay. During the influenza epidemic, the professors of an educational establishment in Denmark were prostrated with the visitation. The children, however, escaped, but at a somewhat singular cost, as it ultimately proved. The authorities of the establishment had been accustomed to weigh the children at frequent intervals, for the purpose of preparing physiological statistics, and it was found that during the epidemic they ceased to increase in weight. Whilst they one and all escaped seizure, their vitality seemed to expend itself in resisting the attack, and they had none left for growth. And in the same way the force and strength and vitality of those who have not truly passed into the kingdom, seems to waste itself in a fruitless and heart-wearying conflict with the evil that is in themselves and their surroundings, and they fail to grow up into the fulness of the stature of Christ's triumphant perfection.

In the highest type of man trained under the limitations of the Old Testament dispensation there is an inferior power of spiritual benefaction. He has no such wonderful message to deliver, and no such unseen helper to attend and crown his word. The Baptist's converts were stirred for a time, but were not spiritualised. Believers in Jesus not only receive His baptism of power, but share through their union with His person His mighty baptismal work. They are the rivers and fountains in which a sin-soiled and weary world is to be washed and find resurrection to a better life. The lowliest Christian in whom the spirit of Jesus dwells is a greater benefactor of his race than the most illustrious toilers outside the kingdom. To communicate the Spirit, by believing prayer to bring men under His sacred power, to wield through mystic fellowship with Christ his prerogative of ministering the higher baptism, constitutes a sublime greatness of which the righteous men of old never thought.

Jesus could not directly preach Himself and His own title and office and work, but did strangely emphasise the high privileges to be possessed and the rare distinctions to be reached by all entering that kingdom He came to found.

CHAPTER XIII.

OUR LORD'S IDEAL OF PRAYER.

IN His discourse on the Mount, after warning against the prayer that is wrong in motive, Jesus goes on to inhibit the prayer that is mistaken in method. Prayer may sometimes bring down but a stinted blessing, or, indeed, be entirely barren, because it is defective in aim, temper, knowledge. The prayer of the secret chamber must be informed by right views of God and of the freeness of His grace, unless it is to be as disappointing as the ostentatious prayer of the synagogue or of the street corner. The spirit of pietistic pride did not flaunt itself before men only, but courted God's favour by a redundant religiousness. Men's prayers, no less than their characters, need the pruning knife, and morbid excesses must be thinned away if there is to be a due degree of fragrant and satisfying fruitfulness. "Use not vain repetitions, as the heathen do."

Our Lord's familiarity with the genius of heathen worship suggests questions which admit only of conjectural answers. Did He draw His information from the Old Testament Scriptures, and have we here a reminiscence of the frantic cry on Carmel, "O Baal, hear us; O Baal, hear us"? Did the sojourn of Joseph and Mary in Egypt bring them into contact with Egyptian idolatries or with the idolatries of the colonists settled there, and were stories of these days sometimes told in the family circle at Nazareth? Had glimpses of Phœnician temples caught the eye of His eager boyhood as He wandered on the Galilean highlands and strained His vision to north and north-west, and had He asked about the services celebrated there? Had Greek and Roman temples on the western horizon, backed by the thread of silver sea, awakened a pitiful interest in His young heart, and had the characteristic rites observed there been described to Him? To what extent had our Lord been a student of comparative religion? He had never entered as a curious visitor even a heathen temple, for He was restrained by the strictness of those Jewish customs to which He was always loyal when no principle was sacrificed. After taking up His abode in Capernaum, He must many a time have looked with pain and humiliation to the roof of a heathen temple which rose high in one of the towns immediately across the lake. From the mixed populations of Galilee He may have heard something of the rites practised there, and of the terms in which the pity of these unheeding images was invoked. At any rate, He had correctly interpreted not only the characteristic note of the worship offered in temples upon which He sometimes looked from afar, but one of the most conspicuous traits of heathen worship through the length and breadth of the known and unknown world. In every pagan religion the repetition of some prescribed form of invocation has been made the rigid condition of power and spiritual efficacy.

There are some things in the devotional life which the Great Teacher could not intend to discourage in these words. The same elementary needs recur day by day, and He Himself taught us to pray for the providential gifts which meet them. Prayer offered under a new sense of need, although it may sound like an echo of the prayer of yesterday, cannot possibly come under the condemnation of Christ's words. In many cases the repeated use of the same phrases may be an intellectual necessity, and the kind friend and comrade of all classes was incapable of reproaching any man because of the poverty of his vocabulary. And we are graciously permitted to repeat those prayers to which no obvious response has come in the way of guidance, illumination, fulfilment. It is only by reverentially reiterated supplication that we can be brought to know God's will, and won into patient accord with its behests. Paul prayed thrice for the removal of the thorn in the flesh. On the night of His passion our Lord prayed thrice, using substantially the same words. The Prophet on the mountain in Galilee is not discrediting the pale, over-wrought suppliant under the gloomy olives of Gethsemane. Not infrequently we may have to repeat our prayers, so that through successive stages of spiritual struggle we may attain the intense earnestness and the prevailing faith which are the conditions of victory. In all such cases, however, the struggle is with our own torpor, selfishness, and unbelief, and with the shadows they project upon our conception of God, rather than with God Himself. Groans and struggles and oft-urged cries are not blamed in our Master's words, and yet it is well to remember that these do not enter into the deepest essence of prevailing prayer. Victory is attained by the climactic moment of faith reached, perchance, through the steps of repeated and persistent wrestling.

It is not sufficient to say that it is heathenish repetition our Lord condemned, or the repetition of those merit-making forms of prayer which had such vogue amongst the contemporary Pharisees. Such practices could only be denounced because of some false principle they embodied.

Why do men repeat themselves in their converse with each other? What thoughts are in the mind of the man who falls into this irritating infirmity in common life? A speaker repeats himself because he assumes his hearers are ignorant and inappreciative, or because of the undue sense he has of his own importance, or because of morbid timidity, which, after all, has the closest possible relation to vanity and personal pride. The nervous stutterer sometimes has to thank his own unhealthy and inordinate self-consciousness for the unhappy affliction to which he has become subject. These facts define the lines upon which the interpretation of Christ's words must proceed.

Repetition conveys an insinuation of ignorance or inappreciation against the man who is compelled to listen to it. The laboured tautologies and much speaking of heathen worship are suggested by the character of the gods addressed. There are the voluptuous and self-occupied gods who are absorbed in the excitements of hunting, and harping, and love-making, and need to be recalled to the needs of their suppliants by piteous and unceasing cries. And there are the impassive gods of the higher pagan philosophies, the gods whose existence is like a vague opium dream,—sparks of half-faded consciousness needing to be fanned into fervent and sympathetic sensibility by the worship of unceasing clamour. And there are also gods personifying wrath, malevolence, destruction,—gods hard to appease, and needing to be softened, conciliated, won by perpetual rounds of service. In the worship of such beings, it is inevitable that repetition should have a significant place. Ignorant and unheeding gods must be instructed, apathetic gods must be stimulated, merit must be patiently built up before implacable, despotic, and extortionate gods.

Jesus felt that worship with this heathenish taint in its methods was an insult to the character of His Divine Father. It implied that the Infinite and Eternal love was slow to apprehend, unwilling to sympathise, unready to help. The prayer of vain repetition covertly accused the prayer-hearing God of imperfect knowledge, imperfect sympathy, imperfect grace.

Closely connected with this misconception of God, which gave rise to the prayer of vain repetition, there is the pride of the worshipper in the intrinsic worth of his own prayers. The man who perpetually repeats himself has an exaggerated sense of the value of his own utterances. And the redundancies of a self-righteous worship betray a desire to exalt self and a sense of the worshipper's own competence in the long-run to conciliate God. In the prayer of vain repetition there was no room for grace, sacrificial vicariousness, mediation, the Father's redeeming love in the Son. It assumed that the worshipper, by the patient and punctilious observance of multifarious forms, could put value and saving efficacy into his own service.

Empty reiterations not only ignore the doctrine of grace, but are inconsistent with the serenity of faith. The man who has said something, and tries to say it over again, does so because he imagines at the first attempt he has not said it effectually and well. And there is something not unlike that in heathen worship, and in that semi-heathen mood of soul into which even Christian worshippers are prone to fall. Heathen prayer, with its never-ceasing repetitions, is what the etymology of the word our Lord used implies, —a painful and age-long stammer which never succeeds in saying what it desires to say, and is entirely contenting to the soul. The faith that perfectly pleases God soars into the high assurance that we are heard and accepted, and then there is no need to repeat the prayer. Much speaking is the sign that the highest ranges of confidence have not been reached. Our Lord seems to say, If you can brace yourself to the great spiritual achievement, ask once, and then fix the hope on an all-faithful Father, and stedfastly watch till the answer comes.

The Lord's prayer is almost immediately given as a concrete illustration of this perfect ideal. In those few quiet sentences, colossal in their strength and childlike in their simplicity, there is no sign of fevered struggle, no trace of noisy reiteration, no word caught up and echoed again and yet again, as though it had not quite done its work. We start our children with that prayer, and rightly so, but it needs a rare maturity of faith if it is to be used in complete sincerity and appreciation. Every succeeding clause is like a sceptre of superhuman conquest wielded over some new domain of life. To us

it often seems that we must needs traverse much
ground and review many truths before we can
come into complete and believing communion
with God. But when prevalency is at last
reached, it is reached by the gracious inspiration of a moment, and much speaking embarrassed rather than invigorated the decisive act
of faith.

Our Lord's short prayers were the products
of His own vivid and unbroken fellowship with
the Father. His prayer, as He stood before the
rock-sepulchre of Lazarus, is the best comment
we can have upon His own ideal as set forth in
the Sermon on the Mount. "Father, I thank
Thee that Thou hast heard Me. And I knew
that Thou hearest Me always." Prayer never
reached a sublimer altitude than that, and to
such an assured habit of soul, repetition would
have been a blemish and a blacksliding.

Ideal prayer is suggested by the announcement of a fact to which it must correspond
rather than directly described. "Your Father
knoweth what things ye have need of before ye
ask Him." There is a link of inviolable sacredness between the lowly suppliant and the loftiest
heaven. He is no spiritual claimant of uncertain
antecedents whose rights must be urged through
weeks of argument and persuasion. And the

Fatherhood to be invoked is a Fatherhood of adequate knowledge and sympathy. The Divine pity anticipates the first cry for help. Did the primitive transgressor request the coming of a promised seed to bruise the serpent's head, or were the accents of love's evangel heard before a single prayer for mercy had rent the air? Where is the supplication, for spiritual gifts at least, which outruns God's promise? The Divine Father abounds in knowledge, wisdom, sympathy, eager and timely inclination to help and to save. An apprehension of these facts is the staple of ideal prayer.

The great practical end to which Jesus is seeking to lead His disciples by this protest against much speaking, is an active and a present faith. He seeks to take them away from the superstitions and superfluities of prayer, lest they should be tempted to trust therein. Acts of piety must not be so magnified as to be made substitutes for God's all-sufficient grace. The Master is seeking to constrain His disciples to a conclusion of immediate and whole-hearted trust. If prayer gains no effectuality through its cumulative reiterations, it must prevail through the intenseness of its present faith; and the sublime fact of God's wise and pitiful Fatherhood, which inspires faith, is always with us and in us, if we will but receive it. In the kingdom of grace the possibilities of to-morrow are the equal possibilities of to-day. Much speaking will not create a better God than He who reigns for our help and salvation in the passing hour. Prayers are heard in virtue of something we are led to recognise in God, and they may reach the climax of their prevalency even now.

It is said to be the property of a crystal to assume precisely the same form into however many fragments it may be broken up. The infinitesimal particle, for the study of which a magnifying glass must be used, is a precise facsimile of the parent crystal from which it came. If we could take God's eternity and break it up into æons, if we could take the æons and break them up into ages, and the ages into centuries, and the centuries into years, and the years into days, and the days into hours, and the hours into moments, we should find each separate moment of God's life to be just as resplendent with benignity, compassion, redeeming grace and helpfulness, as His sublime eternity itself. God's moment is the perfect miniature of His everlasting days.

If that be so, whatever gift prayer can win from God's free mercy it can win at once. It is true, there may be difficulties in ourselves needing time to subdue, but not in God. Looked at from the Divine view-point, faith may reach its meridian now. Before the beat of the next moment has come, it may attain its culminating victory. Our Lord's teaching on prayer is a veiled declaration of the doctrine of present forgiveness, present renewal, present sanctity, present heaven.

It had been said God would answer His people while they yet called, and hear while they were yet speaking. The prayer of vain repetition emptied that evangelical promise of its meaning, and practically made God forswear Himself. It was in the order of God's grace that blessing should come before the hour of prayer had struck. But the Pharisee put the finger on the dial backwards, saying that the blessing would come at a fixed point after the supplication, with due thanksgiving, had been presented and repeated a prearranged number of times. This idea of laboured and merit-making reiteration pushed the moment of blessing into a dim and uncertain future. A systematically measured repetition and much speaking is the devil's doctrine of procrastination engrossed on vellum, bravely illuminated, and smuggled into the ark which is before the mercy-seat.

But does not the fact that the Divine Father

knoweth what things we have need of before we ask Him, prove too much? Does it not imply that prayer is needless, and tend to an ignoble and stupefying quietism? The temptation to restrain prayer because God anticipates our needs, can only come to one who thinks of God in much the same light as the pupils in a famous training school of pickpockets thought of the dummy suspended from the ceiling, out of whose pockets they were to extract as many things as possible whilst minimising to the finest degree their contact with the figure itself. If our object is to possess ourselves of God's gifts, and to have as little as possible to do with God Himself, our Lord's words may perhaps tempt us into languor and spiritual supineness. But prayer is something more than the process by which we make our requests known unto God and God sends doles down to us. The truth that God knows our need before we ask Him, and is prepared to meet it, is announced for the express purpose of quickening the activity of human faith, and not to stultify and displace it. Indeed, by the want of faith we forego our claim for the time being upon the noblest bounties of God's Fatherhood. When our sense of need is penetrated by a sense of God's vivid practical sympathy with it, perfect prayer has been achieved. True prayer is the vision of an open heaven from which stream down supplies that never fail,—rest from every care, help for every frailty, cleansing baptism for every spot, munificent satisfaction for every need.

CHAPTER XIV.

THE PRAYER OF PATIENT STRUGGLE.

IN the Sermon on the Mount, Jesus seems to intimate prayer may prevail at once, and that a swift, simple phrase will give space enough for the assertion of its invincible forces. The thought that we shall be heard for our much speaking dishonours the Father, and must be kept at the utmost distance from our hearts. That stately and carefully conceived sermon is the sermon of superb ideals, abounding in the highest possible conceptions of temper, action, converse with men and fellowship with God. The prayer of disciples made perfect in faith and love will conform to the Master's pattern, and win its prize by a serene believing word. But that short paragraph in the great Galilean discourse does not exhaust all the Master has to say upon the subject of prayer. In the parables of the Friend at Midnight and the Importunate

Widow, He intimates prayer may not always seem to be immediately answered, and He exhorts His disciples to that importunity which is often associated with piercing and reiterated cries.

It may help us to fit these apparently divergent views into one consistent conception of prayer, if we note the side of the subject dealt with on each succeeding occasion. In the Sermon on the Mount He is treating of prayer from the standpoint of God's grace and Fatherhood; the suppliant is a suppliant in his own behalf; and the fulfilment of his request does not conflict with the rights and opportunities of others. In the parable of the Friend at Midnight, he who prays is interceding on the behalf of another, and the children of a sleeping household have to be brought into the reckoning as well as the wishes of one who is anxious to extend some kind of hospitality to a midnight visitor. The subject-matter of the prayer of which our Lord is thinking, in the parable of the Importunate Widow, is the vindication of oppressed and persecuted disciples against those who are doing them grievous wrong, a vindication the urgency of which was one of the strongest motives shaping the disciples' desire for a temporal Messiah, who should execute judgement and righteousness in the earth. Whilst in this case the disciples must continue to pray, the possibility of receiving an immediate answer to their prayers is complicated by the long-suffering purposes God cherishes towards even those who are the enemies of the saints.

That our Father knoweth what things we have need of before we ask Him, may seem to supersede the very need for prayer. Why ask at all if He is never unmindful of us? The answer is obvious. He expects us to ask, so that we may see the imprint of His hand upon the gift which answers our cry. In one realm of His activities He does give whether men ask or not, and the average result is to leave men without a deep sense of indebtedness to His bounty or trust in His presence of personal love. The things essential to the well-being of our physical life are bestowed upon the prayerless and the prayerful alike, sometimes more lavishly upon the first than the second: and what is the moral effect produced? Sun and rain, air and food, home and happiness, are looked upon as a part of our inheritance by natural birth,—a commonwealth of privilege in which every man, be he saint or infidel, has his part, elementary necessities provided in the scheme of the universe, which express no personal good-will of God to the recipients. There are grave reasons why God has to deal with us thus in the kingdom of nature, but He has determined to deal with us by other methods in the kingdom of grace. If spiritual gifts were to be conferred upon any great scale, apart from our prayers and devout expectations, it would have the same unhappy issue. We must be taught by our prayers that every bestowment is direct from His hand. To this end, although He is in sympathy with us before we begin to ask, and has both the will and the power to help, we must receive His choicest bounties upon the unalterable condition of trustful supplication. To manifest Himself and His mighty working in the kingdom of grace, some of the largest bestowments of His love may be kept as the prize of a faith which has stood long testings and grown stedfast through habitual exercise.

It may sometimes happen that the answer tarries when right things are asked, because the requisite faith has not been attained. The disciples are not to be discouraged if they fall below the level of ideal prayer for a time, inasmuch as they must needs reach it through struggle and urgent entreaty, although, after all, the conflict is with something in ourselves rather than in God. The first asking may be faint, inert, soulless, and we must be provoked to eagerness or we shall sink into the languor of a semi-religious fatalism. Some of the blessings of the kingdom may be kept as the crown of persevering prayer; and waiting for God's answer will ripen us into fitness for possessing it. God will give at once all that which we are prepared to accept, keep, and wisely and faithfully use. In asking on the behalf of others, more faith may be required from us than when we ask for ourselves. Some of the precious things in the great Father's treasury may be bestowed only in response to the concurrent faith of His children. When the one hundred and twenty disciples were banded together, in obedience to the Master's word, to pray for the promised power from above, it may be that it was with the dawn of the tenth day only that they reached that spirit of united trust which was the appointed condition of the royal gift lavished to make many rich. Whilst the prayer which obtains for men all the wonder of God's grace may be concentrated into a simple syllable; urgency, fervour, devout doggedness, patient expectations have their moral and religious values in the kingdom of God.

In the background of the two parables referred to lies the thought, that the believing insight into the depths of the Divine Fatherhood, which is the essence of all prevailing prayer, can only be reached after conflict and apparent frustration. God may sometimes appear to a discouraged and shortsighted suppliant in ungracious aspects. In freely working out this idea, Jesus seems almost to forget for a moment the reverence due to His Holy Father, and compares Him in the first case to one who does not touch the highest level of neighbourly kindness, and in the second case to a mercenary and unfeeling judge, who is filling His responsible position for private gain rather than for the ends of public justice.

The disciples will often be assailed by the temptation to think hard thoughts of God, and they will only escape that temptation and see how ill founded their mistrusts have been, by continuing in unwearied prayer. Sometimes He will seem to give but little heed to the intercessions they make on behalf of others. Those intercessions may be prompted by unselfish motives, and may be marked by a thoughtfulness and a sympathy for the outside world which He must surely approve, and yet for the time being no prompt and gracious answer is vouchsafed. And then, again, they may be praying for some act of Divine power which shall vindicate their cause and deliver them from their cruel and unscrupulous oppressor, and God will keep strange silence for long, and look down unmoved upon the turmoil of the world and the woes of His own elect. But to the one who continues in prayer God will at length reveal Himself in His true character, and the enigmas of the past will be made plain. Such importunate prayer may seem like a contention with God Himself, but the future will prove it to be the struggle of disciples to larger and truer views of God. The God whose image presents itself to us in the passing moment of stress and shortsightedness, is not the benign and righteous Being who sits on the throne from generation to generation, and who in the end of things will be found far other than our thwarted, impatient, unbelieving souls have imagined.

In applying the parable of the Friend at Midnight, Jesus refers to the Father's gift of the Spirit, intimating that we must ask it for each other, and that those for whom we intercede must also ask it for themselves. In this case the answer cannot be long delayed. Possibly the Master had in view the time that was to elapse before the outpouring of the Spirit upon those gathered together in the upper room at Jerusalem, and the succeeding interval before the gift of the Spirit to the Gentiles. Redress of the wrong done to helpless disciples by a proud and intolerant world is the subject-matter of the prayer dealt with in the parable of the Importunate Widow. The disciples were even then enduring pain, reproach, persecution for righteousness' sake, and were standing upon the threshold of new and unknown tribulations. Their first impulse was to cry to God against their adversaries, and that was right and fitting, and they must continue to pray. At the same time, Jesus intimates, in the words, "and he is long-suffering over them," that God has saving counsels to fulfil even towards their adversaries. It is parallel with the repeated admonition, "When ye pray, forgive." If God in His fierce indignation had forthwith avenged the wrongs against which His elect were crying, the apostles would have lost their martyr crowns, and Gentile history would never have been turned into new channels by the life and labours of St Paul; and empires to be hereafter rich in saints would have been turned into scenes of waste and ruin. Whilst God listens to the cry of His oppressed servants, He must needs show Himself long-suffering towards their adversaries, and so bring about for His disciples and their cause a more triumphant vindication. The world's sharpest conflicts are, after all, the feuds of children who belong to the same family, and God must declare Himself through matchless long-suffering the common Father of all, and unite them again into one.

Delay brings the crushed and despairing suppliant into step with the Divine counsels, and makes ready the time when his judgement shall be brought forth as the noonday. God gives at last a better vindication than the suitor had ever dreamed. " Smite swiftly ; put the nations in fear ; bring to nought the devices of the adversary," is the first cry rising to the lips of a crushed and bleeding church. But to do that at once would be to rob the world of that glory of forgiving grace which descends upon it from the throne of God in heaven, and to make the swarming continents a vast shambles, slippery with the blood of Christ's adversaries. God is Father of all mankind as well as Judge, and that may keep Him silent for a time. But our continued prayer and supplication will make us worthier children, and will bring us into willing harmony with all the counsels of His Fatherhood, and at last the glorious day of vindication and answered prayer shall come. The Master's only fear is lest His disciples' faith should fail before the hour when He comes to set up His throne. " When the Son of Man cometh, shall He find faith on the earth ? "

The argument of the two parables is from the

less to the greater. If perseverance overcomes the reluctance of a lukewarm neighbour, and constrains him to act against his first impulse, shall it not achieve greater things with the infinite love, and especially when right and acceptable things are asked? If urgent entreaty put a godless autocrat on his mettle, and incites him to that which he did not care to do, how efficacious shall it prove itself with a God who is already covenanted to maintain our cause? There is, of course, a point at which the application of the parable may seem to halt. We cannot thrust ourselves into God's presence, and take His ear by storm after the pattern of these earthly suppliants. But even that power has its parallel in spiritual things, for God can not and will not shut the patient faith of His servants out of His thought.

The parable of the Friend at Midnight is followed by the announcement of a universal law, which brings back the teaching to the ideal level touched in the Sermon on the Mount. "For every one that asketh receiveth; and he that seeketh findeth; and to him that knocketh it shall be opened." That is more than a promise. It is the announcement of an eternal principle in the spiritual universe. There is no fruitless search in the kingdom of God, and no right prayer left unanswered. The answer begins as soon as we pray, although we may not always see to the end of the process, and Jesus knows of no exception to the rule. If we watch the sky for weeks together, we can see the movements of the planets. We detect no movements in the fixed stars, although they may be moving with a mightier velocity than the swiftest of the planets. But seen or not seen, the march of movement is always in progress. We see some answers to our prayers. We can trace God's hand in our lives. In other things our prayers appear unheard. But God is moving no less surely to the answer of our prayers when we cannot see Him, for the law announced by Jesus Christ is always valid and active. The subtle laws by which God answers our prayers no more rest than do the movements of the stars. We are mocked by our shortsighted senses, which tell us God tarries and our prayers are vain.

CHAPTER XV.

CHRIST'S TEACHING ABOUT HIS OWN DEATH.

HOSTILE critics of the Christian faith are accustomed to assert that Paul invented the doctrine of the Atonement, and that it is entirely foreign to the teaching of Jesus Himself. The idea of salvation through a propitiatory sacrifice is an after-thought, and not interwoven with the texture of the simple ethic ascribed to the Galilean Prophet in the original tradition. Even critics within the Church tell us, when we are considering the death of Jesus, " we are compelled to make a choice between His view of the matter and the view which has been subsequently taken." "Certain ideas which have played a great part in human doctrines of the Atonement are not only absent but precluded,"—"ideas in support of which a phrase or two from St. Paul can possibly be quoted."

It may be allowed at once that Jesus did not

define or elaborate a theology of redemption by the death of a substitute; but He said much which prepared the way for the doctrine of the future, and shut up Peter and John and Paul to that interpretation of His death which subsequently dominated the thought of the Church. He was precluded, by at least three sufficient reasons, from giving this all-important article of faith the conspicuous place in His teachings which it afterwards came to have in the writings of the apostles.

Whilst the Master was going in and out with the disciples, they were so lost in their own ideas of how the near future ought to shape itself, that they could not be made to realise the bare outline facts of His death and resurrection. They simply would not bend their minds to that which He was telling them once and again. Anticipations possessed them quite irreconcilable with the statements Jesus was ever making, and they were ready to think His words could not mean what upon the mere surface of the letter they seemed to imply, rather than allow that their old preconceptions were false. If they were incapable of taking in the simple fact of Christ's coming death, they would have been still less ripe for grasping the inner principle by which that mysterious event was in due time to be illuminated and explained.

The complete evangelical doctrine must have its logical starting-point in a historic fact, and could be built up on no other basis. To anticipate the dread issue of the coming months, and make ready a profound and complicated interpretation of what for the present was to the disciples a mere nightmare overcasting the imagination for a moment and then passing away, would have been to invert the natural order of thought and training. There can be no physical science before the universe emerges of which it is the partial solution; neither can there be a science of redemption before the mysterious transaction takes place in which the Divine secret is upfolded.

If He had openly expounded the redemptive significance of His own death, He would have been "testifying of Himself," and would have thus renounced one of His most jealously-kept principles of action. The fact that His death had mystic propitiatory virtues in it, stood in such close relation to His dignity as the Eternal Son of God, and was so vitally connected with His exaltation to the Father's right hand, far above all principality and power, that, had He formulated the inner reason of His own efficacious death, He would have made the world free to accept His challenge and to set aside His claim, inasmuch as He would have glorified Himself. He could not be the herald of His own cross, although to a chosen few He might in some indirect sense be the prophet of it. The setting forth of the magnificent and far-reaching ends achieved by the cross must be left to the inspired testimony of others.

But in His teaching we may find lines of distinct preparation for the truth which was to be declared in due time.

He intimated again and again that the principle of grace, which was hereafter to find its supreme and judicial embodiment in the fact of the Atonement, was almost immediately to receive a larger recognition in God's methods of dealing with men. When the scribes and Pharisees raise the storm of controversy at Capernaum concerning the secret of His power as an exorcist, He intimated that, in healing a nature darkened and convulsed with demoniac madness, He must needs first enter into the unseen strongholds of evil and bind its malignant spirits. The victims of evil could not possibly achieve their own emancipation. The parable of the Labourers in the Vineyard is made to suggest that some other principle than that of mere desert will dominate the coming judgements of God; and he who has earned little or nothing may be found at last to be the recipient of much,—the last being made even as the first, through the unexampled bounty and compassion of the Lord. Those who make sacrifices obtain not the bare market-value of their sacrifices, but "a hundredfold more in the present time, and in the world to come life everlasting." The faithful servants are dowered out of all proportion to their gains. They have but earned pounds and talents with the use of another's capital, and in strict equity have the right to keep only some little proportion of their gains; but they are made "rulers over cities," and "enter into the joy of their lord." The watching servants in the house of the absent lord receive not the payments which are their due, and perhaps some largess to celebrate his festal home-coming, but are themselves strangely ministered to by the master himself. A new rule of beneficence, unexampled in its magnitude, is entering into the Divine dealings with men. The broad forecast receives its definite colouring and fulfilment in the doctrine of the Cross. But the preintimations in Christ's teaching go beyond this. Such language may sound like that of a dreamy and generous revolutionist, yet the law, apart from the traditional glosses upon its letter, must be maintained. Not one jot or tittle is to pass. More subtle forms of transgression are to be judged than any of which the Mosaic code took formal account; and instead of relaxing the ties of obligation, Jesus bound them more tightly than ever. He was at once an apostle of grace and a teacher of law, and these opposite views could only find their last harmonious synthesis in a death which should bring to men illimitable grace upon strictly legal terms.

To the disciples plainly, and to the Jews once or twice in oblique allusion, He foretold the fact and attendant incidents of His coming death, and did little more. If He had started with announcing a doctrine of vicarious sacrifice, and made it the keynote of His teaching, the chief priests and the scribes would have been on their guard against confirming His word by delivering Him for death into the hands of the Gentiles. The predeterminate counsel of God could not, humanly speaking, have been fulfilled. Much as the official classes might hate Him, they would never have given a colour of truth to His teaching by prompting His crucifixion, if it had been a widespread impression that such an event was the key to His after dominion. The earlier intimations of the death forecast for the most part the great tragedy itself, rather than state any doctrine of which it is to be the commanding expression. To disenchant the disciples, and wean them from their dreams of a temporal kingdom, was the first motive of these announcements, and the second was to make them feel in His death a bereavement through the passionate forces of which they should be for ever crucified to the world. He emphasises all the accessories of His slaying, so that the tragedy of the cross might weigh upon them, and awaken thoughts and emotions working through them in the end for their complete regeneration. The external facts must be well marked, for there can be no doctrine of the Cross till men see that a stupendous enigma needs to be explained.

Both before His death and after His resurrection, Jesus refers His disciples to the Scriptures for intimations of the tragedy at which they staggered. From Moses to the prophets downwards, there had been hints of an incomparable sovereignty that was to be attained through pain and sacrifice. Nothing unforeseen had come to pass, and the Scriptures must not be removed from their place of authority, as though they had misled men about the Messiah. And for a yet deeper reason He went back to these Old Testament forecasts of His death. It was the spirit of righteousness which had permeated these writings, binding them into a distinct and coherent literature, which was to be vindicated in results of which His efficacious death was to be permanently fruitful. Although He said little about it, this assertion of the Divine righteousness in the forgiveness of sin, upon which Paul afterwards came to insist so strongly, obviously dominated the view He took of His own work. That work culminated in His death, and those writings which were peculiarly permeated with the genius of righteousness pointed to His death. Upon this subject He shows Himself jealous and intensely sensitive. When Peter, after his great confession, vehemently deprecated the idea that Jesus should suffer and die, the meek and gentle Teacher was roused to the most extreme pitch of excitement ever reached in His career, and denounces this protester against the providential plan of His death as a very Satan of temptation. Jesus Christ had been touched by the hand of irreverent and unskilful friendship in the principles which were most vital to His mission and most holy to His own soul. Simon Peter's position seemed sheer disloyalty to the spirit of righteousness in the Old Testament Scriptures, and was a deadly menace to the enterprise of the Son of Man upon earth. Although so little was said in explanation, the bystanders must have perceived how overwhelmingly momentous our Lord accounted the incident of His own death and its inscrutable issues.

It was not without significance that announcements of His coming death are made in immediate juxtaposition to Peter's bold witness to the Divine Sonship, confirmed as that witness forthwith is by the sign of the Transfiguration. Not only were these special periods chosen that the disciples might afterwards be kept from unmitigated despair, as they recalled the fact that manifestations of majesty were closely linked with pregnant forecasts of His violent and ignominious death, but Jesus meant that, after the tragedy had been enacted, the disciples should be kept from looking upon it as falling under the common category of other deaths, to be explained by the same principles of interpretation. It was a King who had made Himself a servant to die, one who could have declined the ignominy and the pain; and His dying was a supremely wonderful, but a passing incident in a life of glorious immortality. Sharing as He did the attributes of His Father, and possessing His stedfast and unvarying approval, an awful mystery must be recognised in the death which would hereafter be made plain.

If Jesus Christ did not speak directly of His own death in relation to the Divine law, and the regenerating efficacy of His sacrifice is the dominant thought in His brief allusions to the subject, it was for two reasons.

The purest ideals of Jewish law had fallen into desuetude. Its provisions were administered by sufferance only, and the humiliating conditions which invested its precarious enforcement made it unseemly that He should use it as a type or analogy of that sacred and inviolable law whose claim upon the transgressor He was to satisfy in His own death. And, on the other hand, the prejudices of His fellow-countrymen were so strong and bitter, that He could not wisely draw His types and analogies from the precedents furnished by those courts of justice in which the Roman sat. It may be that what is sometimes called the forensic view of the Atonement could only have been duly developed away from the narrow centres of Jewish life, and by one whose free citizenship inclined Him to look with admiration upon the just and unflinching administration of law by the representatives of imperial Rome.

It scarcely fell within the special mission of Jesus Christ, even when He touched in passing upon the subject of His own death, to deal with it primarily and directly as the ground upon which sin was forgiven. His sacrifice had already been accepted on behalf of man before the foundation of the world. In a realm beyond human cognisance that had already taken effect, and He was here upon earth to give visible form and expression to that oblation. Jesus had not to trouble Himself in His incarnate life with the Godward side of His redemptive work. As a Prophet, it was His call to deal with man, and He was zealous for the influence of His future death upon the hearts and lives of His followers. But whilst the relation of His death to the regeneration of those who came beneath its spell seemed to fill the foremost place in His thought, as we construe it through His brief references to the subject, He at the same time explicitly recognises a propitiatory element in His own death; and to say that He thinks of the atonement made by His death as subjective only, is superficial, reckless, and symptomatic of a slipshod knowledge of the four evangelists.

The terms in which our Lord alludes to His death were sometimes imposed upon Him by the thoughts which were occupying the minds of the people, as well as by the more or less rude and imperfect typologies of the past. They were sometimes suggested by subordinate details in the similitudes and allegories He was using. We must not, therefore, expect to find within them that full and final doctrine of sacrifice which those speaking in the larger atmosphere of the apostolic age were free to construct. He spoke of His death as a ransom, because the Jews were looking for emancipation by other methods. The manna and the brazen serpent were employed to illustrate His sacrifice, because these were familiar and instructive incidents familiar to those with whom He was speaking, in which they were prepared to find authoritative instruction. We do not expect from one who teaches by dialogue the exhaustive statements due from the writer of a letter, who can choose his own lines of argument and illustration unrestrained by the interjections of the hearers. When all these facts have been brought into consideration, we can still find in the brief teachings of Jesus concerning His cross the germ of the Pauline doctrine of Atonement.

In one of His early visits to Jerusalem, Jesus foreshadowed the manner of His death and the saving benefits it was to produce, by comparing Himself to the uplifted serpent in the wilderness. The bitten Israelites, looking to that symbol, and taking it as a pledge of God's compassionate counsels, found healing and salvation from the plague. The subject of the discourse in which the metaphor occurs is the new birth, and it naturally fixes the thought upon the dimly predicted death of the Son of Man as a channel of regenerating influence, rather than as an expiation. Nothing, of course, is said in the Old Testament to imply that the serpent was a propitiatory offering to God, but a symbol through which new hope and health followed into the hearts of sinning and suffering men. The obvious interpretation is that the death of Jesus is the cause of new life to those who have the poison of sin in their veins, and are fast hastening to their doom. But it must be remembered that the healing was from the pain of a judicial infliction provoked by sin. The offended God was in the background, and this act of obedience on the part of Moses was based upon God's gracious decree to accept it as a representative expiation. If penalty, moreover, is thought of as innate in the sin itself, to save from sin will be seen to be one and the same thing as to save from the penalty of sin.

In the synagogue at Capernaum, Jesus Christ again dimly suggests the coming tragedy of the cross, speaking of Himself as a God-given bread by which men live, in contrast with the manna in the wilderness which was ineffectual to save men from the capital penalty incurred by the rebellious and unbelieving. These similitudes are perhaps not such as He would have chosen if He had been free to teach an exhaustive and all-round doctrine upon the subject, but were determined by the miracle which gave the keynote to the dialogue. The figure itself halts, for when we eat and drink we assimilate to our own life the substances we receive; but by a believing appropriation of the virtues present in this mysterious Being, in the sum of His redemptive acts, we ourselves are assimilated, and come to share the life and power of Jesus Christ. The death is viewed throughout the entire discussion as a process that transforms us, rather than as a propitiatory act which removes the Divine wrath from the human race. But behind all these representations we can detect an element of law. The manna-eating unbelievers of the wilderness died in spite of the miraculous bounty of which they had been recipients,—died, too, by special visitations of Divine wrath, because the sacramental elements of which they daily partook represented no propitiatory grace. The mystic forces which renew human nature, and make it proof against the death-sentence of God's violated law, take their rise in the act which Christ had in view when He spoke of "giving His flesh for the life of the world." It was His unexampled task to remove from men, by that great event which was yet to unfold itself, the terror and privation brought upon men when the way to the tree of life was barred. He was the Father's gift to the world, and by His own surrender to suffering and death, in harmony with that gift, He was to reverse the doom of death, "tasting," as the apostle afterwards phrased it, "death for every man." He who asserts that there is no hint of the propitiatory element in the language used by Jesus Christ concerning His own death, must surely have forgotten the facts behind the history from which Jesus Christ drew His types and contrasts.

During one of His last visits to the Temple, possibly as He was leaving it on the afternoon immediately preceding His passion, Jesus speaks of the needs-be of His death under the analogy of the corn of wheat which dies to produce its fruit. Here, again, the aspect under which He treats the subject seems to connect the great sacrifice with the quickening of the disciples to newness of life, rather than with the removal of the guilt which rested upon them. This great Prophet of nature tries to make the mysteries of death less staggering to His simple followers, by pointing to the great law of germination as it works in the world, and forecasting a parallel fact which is the fundamental principle of His kingdom. "Do not be dismayed by that which will so soon come to pass, for there are parables of this mystery at your very feet. Like the seed, I must die into glory and fruitfulness, and the philosophy of true progress must find a place for the riddle of death." It would be going too far to formulate a doctrine upon the basis of this analogy, especially when we consider the immediate purpose for which it was used. The dying seed has the power of transmitting its own life to other seeds, and thus the similitude lends itself primarily to the subjective view of atonement. But before we say that such teaching expressly excludes all ideas of Divine wrath and propitiation, we have to ask if the Jewish mind could ever dissociate death from the idea of penalty, and the satisfactions required by a violated law. And then the figure is dropped, and Jesus speaks of "being lifted up from the earth" and "drawing all men" to Himself. By the cross and from His throne He will address Himself to human hearts. He seems to speak, not so much of the expiatory efficacy, as of the soul-subduing power of His oblation. Yet He is lifted up as an appeal to heaven as well as to earth, and it is the Father who both accepts His sacrifice and forthwith clothes Him with the mystery of His attracting power.

On the other hand, another aspect of His

death dominates the thought when He speaks of Himself as "a ransom." In all probability it was the military rather than the Temple associations of the word which were uppermost in His thought, for He had just disclaimed the idea that He came "to be ministered unto" and to restore as a victorious conqueror the throne of His father David. Those amongst whom His lot was cast, and even the disciples themselves, were looking wistfully for emancipation from the Roman conqueror, and the sure sign heralding the Messianic reign would be the rout and destruction of their adversaries. In His early ministry, Jesus had been providentially led to appropriate to Himself the prophetic words which spoke of a national redemption and the coming near of the acceptable year of the Lord. But this loosening of bonds and this recovery of lost birthrights and inheritances must be brought in, not by the fierce magic of an invincible sword, but by the payment of a ransom-price, and that His own life. He was not to be, first of all, a king winning back in battle escheated liberties, and healing deep and rankling woes. A throneless King goes forth to offer His own life for the redemption of His people from a religious thraldom of which the Roman yoke was but an admonitory symptom. Every devout Jew knew that it was beginning at the wrong end of the problem to cast out the proud oppressor; for the Roman was there as a sign of the displeasure of an offended God, and there was no ransom by sword, silver, or statecraft till God's wrath had been turned aside. To some extent the words in which the significance of the death was hinted were moulded by the character of the popular expectation; but Christ's meaning was obvious,—redemption from sin, rather than from those despotic rulers whose dominion was the providential punishment of sin, was the one need of that and of every age; and it was the work of the Son of Man to pay that redemption price, rather than sit enthroned in earthly state.

In the last week of our Lord's earthly life, He adopted the method of instructing by action-parables, a method which appears to have been only once used before, when He set a little child in the midst of the disciples at Capernaum, by way of a sharp and memorable rebuke to their envy and contentiousness. He was about to leave the disciples, and wished to enforce certain lessons after the dramatic fashion of some of the prophets, who, to impress a careless and unthinking age, acted their message. By the washing of the disciples' feet, He rebuked the fatal fault against which He had already raised His impressive protest. By His entry into Jerusalem, He announced His Messianic right and title, and His agreement with the forecast of the prophet. By cursing the barren fig-tree, He brought the doctrine of judgement into peculiar prominence, and declared the wrath which should by and by fall upon all specious and unfruitful things. And last of all, He told the significance of His own death by a modification of the passover rite, which was at once an action-parable and a covenant; and this action-parable, with the principle it embodied, He distinguished from all others, by declaring that His disciples must continue to re-enact it till His coming again. In this solemn and pathetic transaction we must look for a clear and specific indication of the way in which He regarded His own approaching death. Whilst blessing and giving the cup, He speaks of "a New Covenant which is established in His blood," which is "shed for many for the forgiveness of sin," clearly making the removal of human guilt depend upon the offering of Himself as a sacrifice. The words of Jeremiah were doubtless present to His thought. The Covenant announced in the prophecy, of course, promises to bestow a spirit of inward renewal and a law written upon the heart. The subjective view of the Atonement is recognised;

but this side of the question occupies a subordinate and not the primary place. These inward gifts are to be bestowed, because man has been first forgiven and received into covenant friendship with God. And the shedding of the blood is to bring about and to seal this comprehensive remission. Unless the impending sacrifice had a propitiatory significance in Christ's thought, both He and the prophet who foretold the Covenant were egregiously astray in identifying the offering up of that covenant sacrifice with the forgiveness of sin.

CHAPTER XVI.

CHRIST'S TEACHING ABOUT HEAVEN.

IT is somewhat startling to find that He who came down from heaven, and whose special work it was to suffuse earthly horizons with the light of heavenly things, said less about this supremely fascinating subject of the after-glory than His disciples whose writings we possess. The longest connected utterance upon the subject is that preserved for us in the first three verses of the fourteenth chapter of St. John's Gospel. If we were to count up the number of words dealing with this topic, and compare them with the words bearing upon questions of practical life and service, we should find that they form but a tiny fraction of the whole. And yet how clear, firm, illuminating, what a precious heritage to fearful and smitten hearts, the few syllables which dropped from His lips! He never enters into a prolonged disquisition upon this subject, and, with the one exception in His farewell discourse just mentioned, conveys His intimations in swift and passing phrases. The discourse at Jerusalem, in the first year of His ministry, upon the doctrine of the Resurrection, and the controversy upon the same subject with the Sadducees in the last, may be left out of the survey. The Great Teacher sets Himself in those two arguments to vindicate the Divine power which shall reverse the work of death and corruption, but draws the veil over the better and larger life which the resurrection inaugurates for all the true children of God. He implies, of course, that the resurrection uplifts and invests for their new vocation those who are destined to minister before God in the sanctuary of His power, whilst He is silent about the nature of that sacred service which shall fill the deathless ages.

The life to which He bears His brief but emphatic witness is proof against the losses and privations which devastate our present earthly homes. As early as in the Sermon on the Mount, He speaks of a realm in which violence and decay shall be unknown, and where moth cannot waste, rust corrode, nor thief break through to steal, and there must His disciples lay up treasure. And, in the Resurrection controversy, He speaks of the saved people of God as lifted above the shadows of mortality, and made to participate in the pure and deathless state of the angels.

The life of the glorified, as we are able to interpret it through His hints, consists in benign and active ministration. Not only does Jesus declare "all live unto God," but in Perea, and again in the paschal chamber on the night of His arrest, He affirms that, even after the pattern of His own investiture by the Father, He appoints a kingdom to His disciples, and in the coming restoration they shall sit upon thrones of power and judgement. A day or two earlier, He had spoken of a kingdom prepared from the foundation of the world, and of "faithful servants" who were to be "rulers over cities." This language is borrowed in part from the character of the disciples' hopes, and in the form of it there may possibly be a touch of kindly and stingless satire, but the teaching obviously is that the life of heaven shall be a life of wide and unknown power and dominion. It must not be thought of as monotonous, a sunshine that at last wearies with its unchanging splendour, a delight the perpetuity of which produces bluntness and surfeit, a gilded and bejewelled prison of narrow and restricted interests. It will touch large realms in the vast and mysterious universe, and touch them with that note of confidence, authority, dominion, belonging to those whose royal thrones God's hand has set.

Parabolic references to this subject sometimes describe it as a life of hallowed and dignified social communion. The Gentiles coming from the north, south, east, and west, of whom the believing centurion at Capernaum was the type, are to sit down with Abraham, Isaac, and Jacob in the kingdom of God. The glimpse we get of the transfigured beggar, who is in Abraham's bosom, his chosen comrade at a celestial banquet, belongs to the same method of depicting the subject. In one of the introductory acts to the last supper, Jesus speaks of the disciples as eating and drinking like feudatory princes at His table in His kingdom.

And then He refers to the after-life as a life of mystic contemplation, quickened consciousness of Divine and supernatural facts, fellowship with Himself, the Friend and Lover of His people. At as early a stage in the ministry as the Sermon on the Mount, that highest conception of heaven is introduced. "The pure in heart" are to find their perfect blessedness in "seeing God." His own heaven is to be again in the bosom of the Father. "I ascend to my Father and to your Father"; the faithful " enter into the glory of their Lord," participate, that is to say, in the profound blessedness which is the inherent right and prerogative of His own nature. Their cup would be full when they were in the same realm with their Master, and their thoughts and sympathies were interfused with His. The promise made to the disciples is, in its deepest essence, one with that made a few hours later to the penitent thief. "That where I am ye may be also," "with Me in paradise." That is one also with the profound interpretation of eternal life which is strangely interwoven with His high-priestly prayer, "to know thee, and Jesus Christ whom thou hast sent."

And the manifold life suggested in these brief but pregnant hints, is to have its centre and its home in radiant and unnumbered mansions which are gathered within the sheltering vastness of the Father's house.

Several reasons explain the infrequency of Christ's reference to a subject which has such a deep hold upon the thought and hope of the Church.

The first is, that whilst this inspiring fact was always visible in that farther horizon to which He projected His view, He strenuously devoted Himself to the work of the immediate moment, and sought, moreover, by both example and precept, to focus the thought of His disciples upon present and pressing duty. Secularists sometimes assert that the Christian doctrine of heaven has been a clog upon social progress, because attention is diverted thereby from the sore, clamant needs of the hour to some far-off hope. Now, if modern Christians have fallen into that temptation, such was not the case with our Lord Himself. His conception of the work which would most profoundly and effectually benefit mankind was widely different from that of the secularist; but His visions of celestial thrones and crowns and splendours never blinded Him to the need of the meanest sufferer by His side. It was His aim to cure suffering by curing sin; but He never overlooked the fitting occasion for curing either. He was so busy with the moral exigencies of the moment, that He spent His incomparable strength and wisdom in making men feel the sacred constraint of their obligations, and so fitting them for heaven, rather than in painting for their contemplation delightful pictures of what that blessed state should be. And it was only when His work as a Teacher was practically done, that He gave to His disciples the priceless words which brought before them so vividly the glorious life in which He and they should one day be united anew. It was no part of His work to cater for their imaginations.

In the reserve He maintained upon this subject, He was pushing into wider application His great lesson of faith. They were not to be anxious about the things of the present life; and it would be equally hurtful for them to be anxious about details of that better life, brief gleams of which came now and again into His teaching. It was no part of His plan to heal, at one point on the lower side of the nature, the virulent running sore of unbelieving care, and suffer it to break out on the higher. The disciples must trust the Father for the things of a hundred or a thousand years hence, as well as for the bread and raiment of the morrow. The scope for faith would be shut out of their lives if they could be familiarised beforehand with all the incidents and details of the life beyond the veil. Herein lay their finest opportunity for trusting the Father, and trusting the Father's apostle and Son.

It was by His act rather than by his word that Jesus was appointed to bring immortality and all its beatitudes to light. His resurrection from the dead, and His ascension to the right hand of the Father, were designed to suggest it to those who should hereafter interpret the mystery of His work and person. With His bearing away of sin, death itself was to be banished; and when sin and its dire results had passed away, the mind would have no difficulty in conceiving to some extent what heaven was. Heaven is the realm in which God's benign and holy will is done without let or qualification. No language can portray a better heaven than that which we grasp, when we think of the universe as a realm from which the trail of sin is removed, and upon which the unclouded glory of God rests. Christ did more by His acts to bring heaven within the compass of human anticipation than He could possibly have done by the word of His lips.

Jesus felt that if He could give to men spiritual health and healing, they would know much for themselves; and word-pictures, finished with His own supreme skill, would be poor in comparison with that holy vision which would spontaneously arise within them. In fact, He wished to paint the picture by a vital transformation within the soul. With every man who stands in the favour of God, the clear and untrembling anticipation of an ideal life of blessedness after death is instinctive. It was the high task of Jesus Christ to lift the load of sin from the human conscience and to rectify the inward senses, and once that was done the renewed soul would see and feel for itself. It is no part of His task, who gives sight to the blind, to describe for those upon whom the miracle takes place, that which they may perceive for themselves. Whilst the delirium of sin lasts, illusion and obscurity seduce and becloud the mind; but when that is overpast, the vision pierces straight to the heart of what is unseen and eternal. The sense of heaven will be found to be in us, if the darkness and impurity of the nature are removed and the sinner is brought back into the light of God's countenance. Jesus felt the best way of establishing faith in heaven was, not to talk about it, and satiate a curiosity that might turn out to be idle and unsanctified, but to destroy sin and repair the profane and defacing havoc it had wrought in the human soul.

This reserve is further explained by the unfitness of the disciples, and the still more significant unfitness of the multitudes, to understand the ultimate principles upon which the deepest foundation of the glorified state rested. Not only were His brief references to the topic couched in similitudes, but in similitudes largely coloured by limitations inherent in the disciples' thought. In speaking of the future life as one of princely honour, festal gladness, power, dominion, high estate, Jesus, whilst describing realities, clothed them with language not altogether dissociated from views of the kingdom of God upon earth that were half-true and half-mistaken. Teachers, less Divine in their wisdom and sympathy than Jesus Christ, sometimes start meteor-wise mid-heaven, and attempt the description of wonderful things by no means intelligible to their hearers. That was not the method of our Lord. He ever placed Himself alongside His hearers, and moved quietly upwards from their standpoint, seeking to take them with Him by easy steps in His sublime and holy flights. The language of Jesus shows traces of many modes of thought and speech current amongst the disciples. Hence the figurative element in these passing glances at the heavenly life. When the uplifted moods of His hearers left Him free to do so, Jesus portrayed the life of heaven from the standpoint of the interior consciousness. It was spiritual knowledge, love and its high fellowships, eternal life. His references to the glorified state could only be appreciated by those who had in themselves the beginnings of a new experience, and looked at that state from this inner and essential standpoint. It was all but useless to represent heaven by metaphors that would soon need to be taken to pieces again and readjusted and built up anew on a basis of more exact, rigid, spiritual truth. Indeed, the disciples themselves were living under conditions of rapid mental transition, and the heaven that satisfied them now would have lost its spell in a few months or years hence. Jesus could only suggest this heaven by going back to the deep and enduring principles that underlay and determined their friendship with Himself. For the moment, in His farewell discourse, Jesus falls back again upon pictures, similitudes, poetic adumbrations of an infinite hope which might well seem to belong to a simpler and more elementary stage in His teaching. This glimpse of a Father's house, with its bright, clustering mansions, seems almost out of place in a gospel which brings together the more subtle and elaborate discourses of Jesus Christ. But the Great Teacher is melted by the urgent tenderness of His parting; and if the disciples are to be for a time little homeless children in the world, He will speak to them as a child to children. Should it be necessary to go back to rudiments, similitudes, word-parables, so that He may comfort them and make them understand, He will bow Himself to do it. But the fair and far-spreading mansions are dismissed with a word, and He comes back to what for every true and loving disciple is the core and substance of all felicity and blessedness, and will be still more so in the future, communion with Himself. He and they will by and by be gathered into the same world; and such a prospect must surely awaken and draw out the hopes of those who have been His companions for three years past. The presence of the Man of Sorrows in a gloomy, hostile, panic-stricken world had never failed to infuse sweet contentment and holy peace. With what untold rapture and magnificence, then, must that life be replete which is spent in a more perfect world, and overwatched by the presence of God's glorified Son, the Prince of the kings of the earth!

And a few minutes later, when He can turn from the disciples and their cramped ranges of thought, and lift His eyes to heaven, He comes back to His own high keynote, and speaks of heaven, not as a place, although place it must be,—for we cannot conceive of state apart from place,—but as a state first, and a state which can determine its own place. "This is life eternal, to know thee the only true God." The best conception that His own mind can frame as He prays, is that of a conscious, illuminated, soul-feeding fellowship with the Father through the Son. Perhaps the purest natural joy of which we have experience is that which arises out of our knowledge of common things. The knowledge of God is the rare inner essence of all other knowledge; and the immortal joy which springs from it is the sum and infinite expansion of all other joy.

Faith must be allowed its place in facing the problems of the future life. For the time being the disciples are required to depend, not so much upon what they can see and feel and apprehend, as upon what their Master knows. With humble, pathetic, painstaking persuasion, He solicits their trust in His personal truth and fidelity. "If it were not so, I would have told you." The fact that Jesus never repudiates the hopes which rise within the heart of Peter and James and John, and in our hearts no less, is a proof that should content us, for Jesus is one who never misled a follower, even by silence.

The avowal "I would have told" you assumes Christ's competence to speak. His eye had long travelled beyond the ranges of time, and it is just as clear when turned towards the future as when reading the hidden things of the past. At every step He had proved His own faultless knowledge of the work He was sent to do on earth, as well as of the latent characteristics and slowly opening careers of His various disciples:

and of His own appointed work in heaven, and of the parts the disciples shall one day come to fill there in association with Himself, He has the same unerring foreknowledge. The world into which He is about to go is familiar to His eye; for He came from it, and He sees what that world will be when His own right hand has fitted it to the needs of the disciples He has loved and befriended on earth.

Could He betray His simple comrades? Was it like Him to let them feed on roseate illusions only to be mortified at last? He had often risked losing their love, by trying to wean them from false views which would surely have victimised them in the end. The homeless Prophet, by His unpleasant candour, had turned back many a would-be follower; and if He is to be a homeless prophet in the hereafter, He would disenchant His most fervent devotees. He was no man-pleaser, and had many a time dispelled illusions dear as life to His followers. Of course, He did not enjoy crossing the hopes of His fellow-countrymen at large; still less did He like to cross His loving disciples, but He would do it a thousand times if truth demanded. Almost in the same breath, He foreshadows days of persecution which are in store for those who bear His name. Whilst they are under His guidance they shall cherish no false dreams; and if this hope of a glorious and triumphant hereafter is unreal, He will blast that too. Although He had said comparatively little about heaven, they might safely argue from His silence, and draw the largest possible inferences. "If it were not so, I would have told you."

His words had been few, yet it was implied in everything He had done and was about to do. If it were simply to fit men for a temporary citizenship, He would not take such pains to rehabilitate human character. It was for no transient benefit, measured in the fleeting terms of human life, that He was about to bear the unknown curse, and then pour out His soul before the Father in age-long intercession. He had set Himself to give to the deathless conscience of mankind a priceless freedom from its guilt and pain. To make the disciples meet for a nobler and more enduring history than any of which they have dreamed, was the patent aim of His unwearying toil.

Upon these new realms, where the disciples will one day foregather, there is to be the fine sympathetic touch of the Lord's own hand, for it is He who prepares the place. A few days before, on the Mount of Olives, He had spoken of a kingdom prepared for the faithful before the foundation of the world. The principles of that kingdom had been already determined. Its throne was established, its laws laid down, its foundations settled. But the kingdom required adaptation to needs and solicitations which only Jesus could adequately interpret through His own life in the flesh. He had been the Mediator of the original creation, but was now about to set Himself to a sublimer and more difficult task. The kingdom was to receive its supreme elaboration from a hand tremulous with the passion of rich human ideals and sympathies. Why these ages of slow preparation are needed is a matter which sometimes excites our wonder. Could not this realm of glory be summoned into being by a fiat swift as the lightening? The slow preparation and patient upbuilding of the first universe is replete with suggestion. The scientist speaks of "concurrent adaptation," and tells of the huge epochs needed by the manifold parts of nature to grow into mutual fitness and co-operation. And in heavenly, as in earthly things, the perfecting of the place goes on step by step with the perfecting of its inhabitants. A law of patient and comprehensive adaptation is at work. "I go to prepare a place for you." He who made His abode with us, and who still lives in us by His Spirit, knows our needs; and the trust we have in His power and fidelity will fix the range and measure the worth of our hope. Perhaps the writer of the Epistle to the Hebrews had these farewell words in view when he spoke of Jesus, not as the Priest only, but as the Forerunner of His people. Just as the Baptist came to make ready for Jesus Christ, and then turned aside for a moment to greet Him in whom hope was fulfilled, so Jesus is the Forerunner of His disciples, going before them in humility and love, not to enjoy an unshared triumph, but to make ready for all who follow in His steps. Those who pass within the veil see signs of His handiwork, and know that with infinite tenderness and knowledge He has fitted everything to their most complex and delicate needs. Just as a competent art-critic, before he has looked at the signature on the canvas or glanced over his catalogue, will recognise the painter of a picture by his characteristic qualities, so in the Father's home on high every elect soul will see and know at once that the marvellous, skilful, all-adaptive hand of Jesus has wrought there, and wrought for each member of the glorified household; for no other hand could have moved and moulded so tenderly and discerningly. The great law of concurrent adaptation has been at work, and one and the same transforming process has passed upon the unknown realms of light above, and the heirs of the kingdom below who have been ripened through simultaneous activities into wisdom and sanctity.

The social element which appeared in some of Christ's earlier side glances at heaven reappears in His last discourse to the disciples. He had spoken of banquets, the communion of saints of all epochs, deep and sacred affinities, friendship between Abraham and the believing Gentiles. He speaks yet again of mansions where friends and families may meet once more in tranquil love. James and John may be much together then as now. Elect souls shall consort with kindred souls. No cabals, partisanships, envious prejudice, as in the days of old, but many mansions extending their ample and glowing hospitality to every type of mind and personality,—the largest possible diversity of life without the faintest suspicion of schism. Yet although the ideal home-life will be revived and sanctified, and may be even now a symbol of much to be found in heaven, the great central fellowship is with the Lord Himself. "That where I am there ye may be also." Through all the vicissitudes of the last three years they had been with the Master, sharing His life and privilege and power. And He who had admitted them to community with

Himself on earth, would not keep them at arm's length in the richer and more perfect life in heaven. In fact, within a few short hours He showed the sincerity of His promise by pledging His companionship in paradise to one who had hitherto been far even from discipleship. They are His little children, and in this last discourse He has called them so again and again; and just as the head of a family would think the family life incomplete whilst the little children were scattered hither and thither, some pinched with want, some convulsed with pain, some haggard with struggle, some in gloom through stress of temptation, so Jesus will never think of His own heaven as perfect till His little children are gathered there. "That where I am there ye may be also." To be with Him and see His glory is one with seeing God. And it would be the disciples' heaven, as it was His, to see the face of the Father, and through His mediation make their everlasting shelter in that bosom where the Son had once dwelt alone.

CHAPTER XVII.

CHRIST'S VIEW OF RETRIBUTION.

THE large place filled by the doctrine of final retribution in the teaching of our Lord, is recognised by comparatively few modern thinkers. They have so much to tell us about His unique revelations of the Divine Fatherhood, and of the spirit of love He brought into the rigid theology of the Jews, that they are in danger of assuming He said little of serious import respecting this grave and forbidding question. But Jesus spake of that judicial pain and final abandonment, about which modern theology is so reticent, five times as often as He lifted the veil which hides the life of the glorified in heaven. The teacher of the passing hour is apt to be silent about this mysterious and unwelcome topic, and he who gives it a large place in his message is pronounced harsh and old-fashioned. Men treat religion as though it were one of the soul's luxuries and nothing more, and demand that it shall be made altogether pleasant to the taste. The Prophet of Galilee was gentle and richer in pitiful instincts than any member of the race whose headship He assumed,—delighting to speak of the broad, faithful, all-forgiving love of His Father, finding in growing lilies and carolling birds and warm smiling skies the expressive ideographs of a providence always kind,—and it could not be entirely congenial to His tastes to speak of these sad, terrifying last things. He did not take a semi-malicious pleasure in appealing to men's fears, as harsh and bitter preachers sometimes seem to do; but a sacred necessity was laid upon Him. He saw all the mischief which was hidden in sin. He was a discerning witness to the burdens it was everywhere laying upon human life. He pierced realms of judgement to which common men were blind. And He felt profoundly that human nature must sometimes be addressed through its fears as well as through its affections.

On this, as on many other subjects, the Master's teaching was tinged by metaphor; but we must never assume that a metaphor is vague and volatile, with no solid reality of truth behind it. The use of metaphor was imposed upon Him, perhaps, to some extent by the very education through which He had been compelled in His childhood to acquire the speech and modes of thought current amongst men, and certainly by the mental condition and training of His hearers. He could not invent His own language, for that would have put Him outside the circle He wished to influence, and have made Him a speaker in unknown tongues. He had to take the current speech as He found it. Similitudes are necessarily material, and we must not allow the figures of the Great Teacher to lead us to the conclusion that His views of punishment were necessarily materialistic. Penalties may await the bodies as well as the souls of the wicked at their resurrection from the dead; but we cannot say what those penalties will be, for Christ varied the colour of the word with His special illustration, and did not intend to teach decisively upon that aspect of the question. But it would be equally fallacious to say that, because the language is figurative, there is no core of sharp and soul-terrifying reality behind the ominous drapery of the illustration. To say that the king's executioner is a stage make-up of braiding and blazonry, and that, when he lays aside his trappings, there will be no sinewy arm behind them for the fatal blow, might be a perilous inference in an Eastern land.

Some of the metaphors were coloured by those

conceptions of the Messianic kingdom under which Jesus described the advent of His own person and the establishment of His authority amongst men. That He was God's anointed King, was the one thought which first entered into His consciousness when He began to realise His own special work in the world, and from that thought arose His sense of the other relationships which He filled, both to God and to men. It was a necessity of His earthly training and history that He should teach the doctrine of final retribution from this standpoint; and because of the Messianic expectations entertained by the people at large, it was the only way in which He could communicate to them intelligent and impressive convictions upon the subject. The last punishments of sin are often set forth as though they were inflicted by the authority of the new King the Father had established over that spiritual commonwealth founded amongst men.

Jesus intimated that one of the first things to be learned about the kingdom was that it had not been set up for bringing promiscuous vengeance upon the Gentiles. Those who claimed birthright in the kingdom, without fulfilling its precepts, would be as strictly punished as those who did not possess even a nominal relation to it. There would be redress at last for every wrong; and to the man irretrievably blemished in spirit and in life, the founding of the kingdom would be an omen of disaster. The kingdom was not a mere display of force against non-Judean races, but the incarnation of an authority which should execute vengeance upon wrongdoers in the elect nation itself. In the Sermon on the Mount, the Great Preacher intimates that the kingdom had its court of minor judgement for one who nursed wrath against his brother, its council armed with punitive power before which the reviler of his fellow-man should be arraigned, its gehenna of fire into which he should be plunged who had spoken of man in terms of unqualified and profane disdain, and forgotten that which was Divine within him. In the same discourse, He goes on to speak of punishment by fine, and of long, hopeless imprisonment; which figures obviously suggest varying degrees of punishment. Elsewhere He speaks of scourging, of slaying by sword, of cutting in pieces, of punishment by avenging armies, of exclusion from the royal banquet spread for the friends and followers of the King, of repudiated claims to relationship, —all of which things have their counterpart in that new era of moral government Jesus had come to declare and to work out. Under His dominion the degrees of punishment would be just as varied as under that system of dual administration and graded judgement which existed around Him, and in which, of course, the Roman Government played the chief part.

Some metaphors Jesus drew from the inspired records of the past, and in this sense history was to repeat itself with a profounder significance, and upon a more impressive scale. The flood which swept away the reckless, sensual, idolatrous antediluvians; the tempest of fire which burned up the vicious Cities of the Plain, with their rotten æstheticisms, making the after-generations sicken and shudder at the thought of their doom; the invasion which dismantled Tyre and Sidon, and turned them into defenceless, poverty-stricken fishing hamlets; the stern judicial discrimination which passed by all the loathsome and outcast lepers of a century but one; the avenging sovereignty which laid drought and famine upon the length and breadth of a land polluted with idolatry, whilst one poor widow upon the frontier found exemption from the miseries of the rest;—all these judgements were to have their terrible analogues and parallels in the new era of the Messiah.

Contemporary disasters and tragedies, the ailments and misadventures of the common people, furnish another set of similitudes. The fate of those upon whom the tower of Siloam fell, to crush and mangle and destroy; the ruthless slaying of the Galileans in the Temple courts, whose blood was mingled with that of their sacrifices,—suggest woes which will overtake those who think themselves better than these ill-fated victims, and who, neglecting to present the offering of contrite spirits, vainly trust in the Temple sacrifices to shelter them from the wrath to come. The life-long paralysis caused by sensuality is looked upon as the type of that degradation and living death which will overtake the souls of those who lack moral courage and continue in sin. The coming of the thief, which works mischief to property and life, is like the sudden advent of the Son of Man to those who slumber and are unprepared. The impoverishment and sudden death of the Rich Fool are made to hint the dire spiritual privation which will one night overtake those who are not rich towards God. The wreck of the ill-founded house is made a symbol of the futility, mortification, and catastrophe which will engulf the hopes of those who do not begin and continue their lives in the spirit of obedience to the sayings of the Great Teacher sent from God.

Our Lord's teaching upon this subject was

sometimes coloured by the metaphors of common industry. Those who lose the savour of spiritual things, once in them, shall be like the deteriorated salt, which is held valueless and is cast out to be trodden under foot of men. Here the figure of the fire occurs again; and such is the frequency with which Jesus returns to it, that it seems to have some special and outstanding significance in setting forth the doom of those who have brought upon themselves the last condemnation of God. We see the fire kindled on the lake-shore to destroy useless or unwholesome fish. We hear its flames crackling amidst the vineyards and olive groves of Ephraim and Judah, as the husbandman brings his load of dead twigs, unfruitful branches and blighted trees, to be consumed, hoping that the pest which has settled upon them will finally disappear. We see the columns of smoke ascending from the gathered harvest fields, where the hired servants are crowding on chaff and stubble, thistle and weed, and hated tare. And the picture has its counterpart in the end of the world. For those who, after all the toils and benign enterprises of the kingdom, are persistently unfruitful, a doom of this type will be reserved. The similitudes which mirror these truths are homely and passing, but there is a core of soul-terrifying fact in the figurative presentations of that doctrine of retribution which, in one shape or another, is universal as the conscience of mankind.

One of the most obvious traits of Christ's teaching upon this subject is, that there are gradations of judicial pain, and that these are determined according to the complex influences which enter into the life of the transgressor. Whilst sin in the abstract is one and the same, and divergent types of sin have a common germ of virulence, the circumstances under which sin is committed may be more or less aggravated, and sin may be either a transient aberration or an ineradicable habit. And if the conditions under which sin is committed vary, the punishment finally meted out to it will be equitably proportioned. We have raised not a little of the difficulty which gathers around this subject, by making our delineations a silhouette in the same fierce, absolute, and untempered black. Hell will mean diverse inflictions for those immured within its impassable gulfs. The council before which Jesus declared the implacable man should be arraigned, administers a milder cone of punishment than that implied in being thrust into the gehenna of fire. There are "the many stripes" threatened to those who had knowledge of the Master's will, and "the few" awarded to those who did not sin against such light. There is a being "broken in pieces" for the man who makes Jesus "a stone of stumbling," but a being "scattered as the dust" for him upon whom avenging wrath alights. A servant of the Lord may be sufficiently punished by the forfeiture of his pound, whilst a rebellious enemy, who appears in the background of the same parable, active and quenchless in his hates, must be slain with the sword. There are benighted and pleasure-loving idolaters from Tyre and Sidon, and brutal sensualists from the Cities of the Plain, whose lighter doom will be coveted by the proud, hard, impenitent souls of the lakeside towns who received the gracious words of Jesus in vain. Such passages must not be interpreted in either a temporal or a purgatorial sense, for they represent a last judgement beyond which the consciousness of Jesus, as far as we can interpret it, discerns no returning gleam of light or hope. There may be different degrees of punishment without the terminability of the pain or the commutation of the sentence. Two inmates of a hospital for incurables may each have twenty years of pain before them, and may suffer in widely different degrees. To be cast out will be a sufficiently bitter doom to the one whose burden of judicial pain is the lightest of all; but it is a conception fraught only with mischievous rudeness and inequity, that God's gloomy prison-house has precisely the same scale of tribulation for every soul hurried through its iron gates.

Christ's teachings upon the subject of retribution range themselves into three groups,—positive, privative, and innate penalties.

Some of the woes He depicts alight upon transgressors by the direct act of God or His messengers. And these woes are described as fastening, in part at least, upon the body and its sensibilities. We call these materialistic views of punishment, and there is a tendency to exclude them entirely from modern eschatology. The colouring in Christ's words may belong to the metaphors rather than to their essential substance; but if the wicked are to be raised from the dead at all, it is scarcely rational to assume that the range of punishment will be limited to the spirit. The Master speaks of a casting of "the body," as well as of "the soul," "into hell." There is the scourging which was a punishment inflicted by the rulers of the synagogue upon petty offenders against the ordinances of religion. Then there is that slaying with the sword which belonged to the supreme authority, and was directed against capital crimes. The stone itself strikes. And there is the casting into a fire whose flames can never be quenched, an expression sometimes used without the preamble of a metaphor. In an unspiritual age these conceptions of punishment could scarcely be omitted from a ministry which was to touch all classes of the community.

Some of the punishments are described as privative. Favour and forgiveness are permanently withdrawn when they have been wasted and misused. The Son turns with shame from those who were ashamed to acknowledge their benefactor in His humiliation, and will not confess them for friends in the presence of His Father. The spiritual gifts represented by pounds and talents are for ever withdrawn from those who were once distinguished by their possession, and the possibility of honour and eternal glory is foreclosed. Those who stood first are put with the wretched and outcast stragglers in the ranks of humanity. The door which admits into the presence and splendour of the King is closed never to be opened again, and those outside are shut off from the peace and blessedness which abound where He unveils His glory. "He that committeth sin is the servant of sin, and the servant abideth not in the house for ever." In these representations it may perhaps be seen that positive penalties are often dealt out to the foes of the King, whilst the privative penalties bring untold bereavements and desolations to those who have once been servants but have proved faithless.

The penalties of the last judgement are sometimes described as innate or self-inflicted. Men, after all, have been seeking their own doom. In their perversity and wilfulness of heart they rush against the foundation-stone. The growing light of the evangel brings hidden sin into view, and stirs up self-reproach and condemnation in those who had been trusting to the thick darkness. An inward worm restlessly gnaws at the throbbing centres of the life. The word spoken rises up to judge men in the last day. There is a sense in which all penalty is self-inflicted, and these passages in the Lord's teaching do but present another phase of the subject. Our ignorance of the inner history of evil, and our inability to estimate the degree of light against which sin is committed, obscure the fact that in every case the punishment of sin is really self-inflicted; for to a far greater extent than we know, the punishment was seen, reckoned with, and defied in the very act. It may be one of the motives of the last judgement, to show not only that God takes direct part in the punishment of sin, so that He may vindicate His own righteousness, but that the impenitent sinner has his part also in this judicial work, and in every case has punished, and will continue to punish, himself.

The feeling of the present age, or it should perhaps rather be said of the present hour, sets strongly against all conceptions of punishment. We seem to have acquired our Lord's recoil from the pain that vexes and overshadows human life, without learning that principle of righteousness which asserted itself in His spirit and teaching, and we subordinate the principle to mawkish, overgrown, unreasoning sentiment. We refuse to think of punishment as an assertion of righteousness, and contemplate it as hideous suffering and nothing more. The result is that we practise every kind of misleading slight upon the reason, and land ourselves in a position in which it is impossible to justify the enforcement of law, either in this life or the life which is to come. This capriciousness shows itself in trifles. We loathe the hangman, and at the same time we honour the judge, of whose behest the hangman is the instrument. Apart from the difference of education and private character, the one man may be just as good as the other; for it is not more dishonourable to pinion a murderer and draw the bolt of the trap-door on which he stands, than to put on the black cap and pronounce sentence of death upon him.

Many ideas are rife amongst us which burst like bubbles when frankly reasoned out to their just conclusions. Privative, but not positive, penalties may be reconciled with the beneficence of the Divine character. The dogma of materialistic punishments is an outrage upon the enlightenment of the age; but it is not quite so objectionable to believe that God may have spiritual pains in reserve for the punishment of sin. The Divine character is held to be free from reproach if nature punishes a man for any transgression of its laws, or if a man punishes himself by his unconquerable shame and remorse: but it is barbaric to assume that God will visit sin by direct and terrific acts of His own power. These distinctions rest, however, upon no logical foundation, and are the mere whims and fashions of a fitful and unreasoning temper. The same deep doctrine of punishment is presented in these many-sided metaphors, and Jesus Christ was not giving us alternatives for the form in which we must elect to hold the doctrine, when He looked at the judgement of sin from these divergent points of view.

All positive pains may be described under

privative aspects. Positive penalties are simply the processes by which pre-existing conditions of well-being are taken away. To have sealed up the air passages in the chamber in which the young princes of English history were slumbering, would have had precisely the same result as smothering them by the hand of the ruffian. Such a method of destroying life would have been more ingenious and less revolting, but the moral quality of the act would not have been affected one way or the other. To withdraw the presence of the King is one and the same thing with thrusting into the outer darkness. To take away the grace that gives the promise of liberty from sin and its condemnation, is one and the same thing with binding in fetters and appointing to the soul a portion with hypocrites and unbelievers. For God to withdraw His smile for ever, is one and the same thing with leaving a wicked nature to the self-torment of its own bad passions, and to the repulsive associations of its kind. To finally take back the gifts which have fitted for usefulness, is one and the same thing with casting for ever out of the realms whose law is love and whose recompense eternal peace.

Men resent the idea of material punishments, and tolerate a doctrine of punishment whose issues bind spiritual pains upon the soul, for the simple reason that material punishments appeal to the imagination, whilst spiritual pains do not. As a matter of fact, it may be a far less harsh thing to lay stripes upon the flesh, than to goad to frenzy and madness by solitary confinement, even though the solitary confinement is mitigated by soft beds and luxurious diet. Thousands of men would only be too glad to exchange their mental pains for physical equivalents, if the translation were possible. There can, indeed, be no separation between physical and spiritual punishments. We assume they are distinct conceptions, because we have imagined the indissoluble unity of our being broken up into the entities of flesh and spirit with separate currents of consciousness and sensibility coursing through each. If Jesus meant anything by His doctrine of the bodily resurrection, He certainly meant that the unity of man's compound being would be restored. Every spiritual pain ultimately becomes physical, and the converse is equally true; and the only question in debate is whether the pains of final retribution work from the mental centre to the circumference of the personality, or from the circumference to the centre. The issue is not affected one way or the other, and the credibility of this principle in the Divine government is just the same as before.

The men of our age are prepared to believe in retribution of every kind in the order of nature, and to believe, if they have any faith in a personal God at all, that the facts must be found at last to harmonise with His goodness; but they flout the idea of punishment by a direct stroke of Divine power. The vague thought underlying the distinction is, either that God has made nature His hangman and commissioned it to do work He would not Himself touch, or that the antiquity of the retributive mechanisms in nature affects the righteousness of the result,—just as though the killing of a man would be a righteous act if carried out with a weapon made two thousand years ago, but a murder if done with a weapon made yesterday! The distinction is unreal, and ignores that doctrine taught by Jesus Christ of the Divine immanence in all the movements of nature. God is as directly responsible for all the retributive processes in nature as though He did these things by the might of His own unveiled Person, and by the spoken fiat of His lips.

Men sometimes profess to be ready to believe in the punishment a man brings upon himself, but not in that to which God dooms him by some sentence of the judgement-day. Yet again the distinction is unreal; for if God has so constituted the human mind that a man inwardly punishes himself in the very act of sinning, God is just as immediately responsible as though punishment were His own infliction and the act of the passing moment. If the word preached to men judges and condemns in the last day those who now reject and disobey it, that is just as much arranged for in the preaching of the word as though God built up the mechanism of punishment before the sight of all men in the very hour when the sentence takes effect. God is not only directly responsible for all the pains and penalties inherent in the complex order of nature, but for the pains and penalties inherent likewise in the moral constitution of man. If He makes a sinner punish himself, He is just as responsible for it as the owner of a garden is for the mutilations, through spikes and broken glass, the robbers of his fruit and flowers have brought upon themselves. The spikes and broken glass he had meant for warnings, just as God means for warnings everything He has told us about the deadly effects of sin, but the transgressor himself changes the warnings into penalty and enduring woe. When the secrets of all hearts are made known, it will be seen that sin is, and always has been, and ever will be, self-punishment, whilst the truth at the same time holds that it is punishment no less by the direct act of God. For those who have become callous, and who seem incapable of punishing themselves, the Divine act of punishment may consist in reviving by a breath the power of punishing himself, once inherent in man's moral nature.

In our Lord's teaching, there is no intimation that the death sin bears as its last fruit is the cessation of consciousness. That would be no punishment, but rather salvation for every man who has sinned, inasmuch as every man who sins without repenting becomes at last loathsome to himself. To four hundred millions of Buddhists, the cessation of consciousness is thought of as a goal to be striven for through long discipline and prayer. Can it be that the Buddhist's paradise was the place of punishment in the scheme of Jesus Christ? If death, which is the penalty of sin, is the fading away of personal consciousness, it cannot be better to pass through life maimed than to enter this mild kind of hell with two eyes and two feet.

For those, at least, who had light and teaching in the present life, no prospect of an effectual repentance in the world to come is held out. The shut door does not open again. No herald of glad tidings appears to the belated and forlorn, who are gnashing their teeth in the outer darkness. The King does not come out and entreat the sullen guests as the father in the parable entreated the churlish son. As far as we can judge the contents of Christ's consciousness from His message and the spirit of His message, no faint vision of a far-off repentance mitigates His grief for those who sin away the high privileges and opportunities of the present life. "Ye shall die in your sins, and whither I go ye cannot come."

These darker features in our Lord's teaching were not the outcome of bitterness, disappointment, smouldering tempers of retaliation. It is not unusual to find a religious teacher who is upright, sincere, and faithful, as he judges things, begin to deal with the sombre aspects of the truth when his hearers seem stubborn and unwilling to give heed to his message. These declarations of future punishment were not provoked by any ebullition of feeling against the individual. Jesus did not anathematise His adversaries, and promise immunity from punishment to His own followers. These minatory subjects are scarcely alluded to in our Lord's thirteen or fourteen recorded conversations with individuals. Nor are they specially characteristic of the period of His rejection. Glimpses of final punishment occur in the Sermon on the

Mount, when the Prophet of Nazareth was yet in the heyday of His popularity. And menace is always blended with tenderness. In the mind of Jesus Christ these opposite qualities had found for themselves a strange harmony. The denunciation of the privileged cities of the lake-shore is almost immediately followed by the low-breathing gentleness of the wonderful words, "Come unto Me all ye that labour and are heavy laden, and I will give you rest." The sevenfold thunder peal of "woe" in the Temple, when the hour of His final rejection was about to strike, is closely connected with the hope-inspiring parable of the Two Sons, and closes with the memorable expostulation of fruitless compassion: "How often would I have gathered thy children together as a hen gathereth her chickens under her wing, but ye would not." These denunciations of judgement, combined as they are with heart-broken appeal and divinest charity, suggest the similitude of a crater belching through its stony lips destroying fire, whilst a a few feet away crystal springs murmur, vernal flowers blow, and the note of the song-bird is heard.

CHAPTER XVIII.

THE SENSITIVENESS OF THE TEACHER TO HIS ENVIRONMENT.

HOW far was our Lord in the course of His public ministry affected by the vicissitudes of the seasons, the genius of the places in which He taught, the shifting moods of popular feeling? Did the temper of the crowd react in any degree upon His own states of mind, and colour the forms assumed by His instruction and appeal? Can we see the circumstances through which He passed reflected in His dialogue, conversation, and continuous discourse? Are the parables perceptibly autobiographic? If we look carefully we may perhaps see such indications. Whilst in His deeper consciousness essential truths take their rise whose substance never changes nor dissolves, there is at the same time a varying poise of light and shadow determined by the earthly incidents of His ministry.

Jesus Christ is sometimes thought of as a miraculous preaching-machine, and that exquisite, human, mobile sympathy which was one of the secrets of His power is quite forgotten. He was no far-off angel with a passing message, gliding through the atmospheres of earth, impervious alike to their dulness and illumination. He was no mere sign in the heavens, flashing down upon men's eyes, through cloud and through sunshine, counsels and precepts of imperturbable wisdom. We must think of Him as one who was responsive to every subtle breath in His surroundings. In His words we may trace the ups and downs of popular feeling characteristic of the spheres where He wrought. He was sometimes encouraged and sometimes depressed,—when He had receptive hearers led to speak of the love of God and the blessings of the kingdom, and when He was confronted with obduracy and frivolous heedlessness compelled to hide that pearl He was ready to bestow on the poor and contrite. Out of His unity of life with the Father there came into His daily consciousness and teaching elements which were never volatile or intermittent. But this was only one side of the problem. The outline and surface-colour of His instructions were often determined by the temper of the hour, and the suggestions which arose from a sympathetic study of those with whom He was in contact. He shared the jubilation of His returning disciples; and found, in a fallen woman's outburst of penitent love, ample compensation for Simon's slight. He regarded with unfeigned delight the outward virtue of the rich young man who was not yet ripe for the great renunciation, and the candid and discerning scribe He declared to be "not far from the kingdom of God." And, on the other hand, His heart was weighted as with the oppressiveness of a gathering thunderstorm, when He looked upon Judas, sitting with averted eye at the Last Supper; and it was only after the traitor had left that He could speak freely the comforting words in store for the disciples.

In His general teaching we find the ruling characteristics of His environment more or less mirrored in subdued tints. Each locality in which He taught, and each varying period of His three years' ministry, puts its specific mark upon His speech. The temper of those whom He addressed, and even the influences of the seasons, made themselves felt through His discourses. The coldness and the rancour of the priests and scribes, and especially the unresting hostility which confronted Him on every side in

Jerusalem, vivified and accentuated the premonitions He had of His coming death, although the love of His heart changed the premonition to an evangel as it found utterance through His lips.

In the exercise of His ministry, He was just as sensitive as the most human of His followers to the influence of cloud and sun, wind and rain. In describing one of the soul-vexing controversies typical of His visits to Jerusalem, John tells us that "Jesus was walking with the disciples in the porch called Solomon's," when the Jews came to Him with one of their taunting interrogatories, and "it was winter." The interjected comment seems to bring before us the picture of Jesus and His disciples, not too sumptuously fed nor too warmly clad, with faces still stinging with the sleet that has been beating into them during their morning walk to the Temple. They are pinched, blue, shivering, presumably depressed and discouraged, almost cowed by the unkindly elements that are chilling men to the bone and weighting their spirits. And at this juncture the Jews came round about Him, as though finding in His pitiful plight a trenchant refutation of His claim, asking, "How long dost thou hold us in suspense? If thou be the Christ, tell us plainly." The Evangelist perhaps implies that it was an aggravation of these bitter controversies that they should have been forced on the Great Teacher under such conditions, and that the keenness of the winter gave edge to the malignity which beset Jesus Christ on every side. And then after that the Evangelist goes on to tell us that "He went again beyond Jordan into the place where John was at first baptizing." That place was the scene of the opened heavens and of the Father's testimony to His sinless and loving Son, and the Man of Sorrows may have needed to invigorate His spirit by calling to mind these holy memories of His opening ministry. He hears again the echoes of the Father's voice, and the pain caused by the taunts of these unbelievers is assuaged. Those who had felt the force of John's preaching were also to be found in large numbers in the adjacent districts; and after the well-nigh barren ministry in Jerusalem, He needed the consolation which would come to Him from teaching prepared and contrite crowds. And beside all that, the district was subtropical, being many hundreds of feet below the level of the sea, and afforded the refuge needed by the worn and heart-sore Teacher, not only from the wrangles of the priests and scribes, but likewise from the piercing wind and rain which raged about the rocky tableland on which Jerusalem and its Temple were placed. The warmth of the sub-tropical plain seems to pervade the incomparable discourses addressed to publicans and sinners in Perea; and when, in the early months of the year, He crosses the Jordan, and blesses the children not far from Jericho, and makes Himself the guest of the delighted Zaccheus, one feels that He almost carries the fervour and the fragrance of the coming spring in His garments. The short and fruitful stay in Sychar, in the first year of Christ's ministry, seems to reflect the gladness of the harvest-fields around Him, for it must probably be fixed in the month of May. The spirit of the summer seems to be brooding in His veins, and in the bending forms of the reapers around Him He sees prefigured the great in-gathering which shall reward the toils of His disciples when sowers and reapers rejoice together. The Sychar sojourn, following as it does a vexing and contentious visit to Jerusalem, is like lighting upon a magic oasis after a hot trying pilgrimage through the sand and rock of the desert. The sunshine and the blitheful harvesting helped to lift the Great Teacher's hopes, or at least to bring a strange glow into the expression of those hopes. When Jesus made the succourer of the man who had been stripped by thieves a native of this despised province, it may be that memories of these sunny harvest days, and of the goodwill with which He was welcomed, came back to His mind, and He said within Himself, The hero of My parable shall be a Samaritan,—and so the light of this cloudless summer scene reflected itself in a brief after-glow at the end of His working day.

In the course of His public ministry, Jesus often shows Himself sensitive to the genius of the locality in which He was teaching. This point has had but scant consideration in explaining the differences between the synoptical Gospels and the Gospel according to St. John. Something must, of course, be put down to the temperament of the Fourth Evangelist which led him to catch up subtleties unperceived by the rest, or which were beyond their power of intelligent apprehension, and also to the personal colouring with which he invested them in his narrative; but a still more important place must be given to the fact that, in the Temple discourses reported by St. John, the Great Teacher was compelled to adjust Himself to the mental habits and current language of His hearers. The tone is philosophic, the argument profound, the language not infrequently metaphysical. A different mode of presenting His message was forced upon Him by the training, temper, and traditions of the capital. The discourses in the Temple seem to have been delivered in an electric and overcharged atmosphere. We could find that out from the discourses themselves, apart from the explanatory notes with which they are reported. He appears as a disputant and controversialist, and only now and again in the lull of the storm can He get the opportunity of speaking as a herald of good tidings.

He felt that He had before Him, in the Temple, men of a different temperament from those who formed the main body of His hearers in the northern province, and His discourse necessarily took on a different complexion. He could not have rapid success here. Nicodemus and Joseph of Arimathea ripened to faith and friendship slowly, for their traditions were politic and opportunist. He needed followers and coadjutors who were frank, impulsive in the best sense of the word, susceptible to enthusiasms. These city hearers lacked boldness, fervour, generosity, and were the slaves of public opinion: with an interest in religion that was perfunctory, academic, and mixed with prejudice. Jesus knew the weakness of the city character, and its unfitness to bear the stress of persecution, and He did not recruit His bodyguard in Jerusalem or Judea. Judas, the only apostle Jesus chose from the south, was a failure, and worse than a failure. A sense of the incompatibility of His surroundings appears in the discourses, for they lack the gladness and the buoyancy of the teachings linked with His sojourn in the highlands of Galilee, on the lake-shore, or by the banks of the Jordan.

The Sermon on the Mount is perhaps less coloured by the human side of the Teacher's personality, and the public experience through which He was passing, than any of the consecutive discourses which have been handed down to us. That deliverance is marked in many of its passages by the august severity of the Lawgiver, the voice seeming to ring from the spaces of another world, and to convey a sense of majestic detachment from the conventions of place and time. Its early notes are those of pure and high-pitched joy. It opens with an eightfold benediction, with which possibly a refrain of subdued warning was interwoven. In its closing parts it contains solemn forecasts and significant threatenings; but these are directed against the perils of individuals rather than against the disaffection and apostasy of the great masses of the people. In that great official manifesto we see the coming shadows which will all too soon fall upon the ministry even in the northern province of Galilee, and trace the reaction and moral disaster which will by and by be brought about by self-interested and unprincipled teachers. In the climax of His fame and prestige, He saw symptoms of unreality in the applauding multitude which would all too soon bring about the great falling away.

The three groups of parables perhaps mirror more clearly the religious outlook than any other portions of Christ's teaching, excepting, of course, those sections which are put into a definite historical setting.

The lake-shore parables recapitulate in their quiet undertones a chequered history which was already enacting itself. The parable of the Sower has four subdivisions, three of which deal with failure, and only one with success; and although, of course, the total area of wayside, thorny, and rocky ground may have been insignificant in comparison with the fruitful acres, the prominence given to the cases of failure sufficiently shows how the spirit of the Master was grieved and wounded by the facts about Him. Every follower was not a saint; and in the great testing crisis, numbers who had crowded in the wake of the Prophet, and listened with apparent interest to His teaching, would be found unworthy. In the parable of the Sower, the blame of failure is made to rest with the people themselves, who neglected to prepare their hearts for the seed of the kingdom. In the succeeding parable of the Tares, the blame of failure did not rest so much with the people themselves, as with the enemy who put false thoughts and false views into their hearts, and so nullified the virtues of the good seed. The Wicked One was perhaps already sowing his tares by the hand of those who came from Jerusalem to spy out the new movement, and who were now passing furtively through the crowds to slander Jesus Christ and His work, and to contradict those principles He enunciated, which were the very essentials of salvation. In the twin parables of the Hid Treasure and the Pearl, Jesus not only lays down the demand for sacrifice as a condition of complete blessedness in the kingdom, but He intimates that, in spite of discouragements and contrary appearances, men were already giving up all things for the gospel's sake. Whilst reminding future disciples of the obligations resting upon them in pursuit of the supreme good, He at the same time immortalises those who were even now counting all things loss so that they might gain salvation. In the two parables of the Mustard Seed and the

Leaven, He declares His own confidence in the complete triumph of the kingdom, in spite of the fact that there was much to sadden and cast down in the present outlook. The Draw-net which enclosed both good and bad seems to speak again of the mixed results which would follow the labours of the disciples, and of their successors in many generations. Whilst He was teaching by the lake-shore, He could not entirely escape thoughts of those who had listened in vain to His message, and of the unhappy multitudes of whom they were types.

Our Lord's hopefulness seemed to find its most unqualified expression in the three Perean parables of the Lost Piece of Silver, the Lost Sheep, and the Prodigal and his home welcome. In this comparatively remote district the signs of the times were not uniformly bright. It was here He spoke terrible words about the abuse of riches. And as He passed to and fro, finding so many ready to welcome His message of peace, He was not allowed to forget that He was in the territory of Herod, the murderer of the Baptist; and the shadow of the gaunt and cruel tyrant ever and anon fell across His pathway. In these remote regions, too, there were spies from Jerusalem tracking His movements, trying to discount His miracles, confronting Him with cunning and sinister questions, and watching with undisguised scorn the spell cast by His message upon publicans and sinners. But there was a deeper and more widespread contrition here than in any of the places of His previous sojourn, and He was able, not only to forget the hostility of the few, but to respond to the humility and contrition of the crowd with a higher and more sustained note of graciousness and jubilation than He had touched in the ministry of the past twelve months. His pulses are strangely stirred by the frank, impressionable, self-abasing crowds to whom He is speaking; and neither the taunts of scribes nor the ruffianly threats of the red-handed Herod can ruffle the surface of His discourse, or seal up the fountains of His infinite tenderness. We are ready to thank the publicans and sinners whose undisguised and widespread repentance stimulated the Teacher to this transcendent effort, for they so react upon Him that we get such an insight as we have never had before into His amazing compassions.

The parables of the closing days of the ministry spoken in Jerusalem and its immediate neighbourhood, seem to epitomise the vicissitudes and the conflicts of the past three years, and to contemplate with indomitable hope the epoch about to dawn. Over all these last parables there lies the purple shadow of His own terrible death, and yet perhaps their tone is more sanguine than that of the Galilean parables, and the victory of the truth has a larger place upon His canvas. The parables of the Two Sons, and of the Wise and Foolish Virgins, whilst spoken as warnings, yet imply larger issues of good in the great reckoning than the parable of the Sower. In the parable of the Talents, those who are diligent and faithful outnumber the slothful. The slighted invitations to the wedding feast, and the filling up of the place with others, as well as the taking away of the vineyard from the rebellious husbandmen, and its lease to worthier tenants, seem to imply that the failure which has pierced the heart of Jesus Christ in His personal work as a Teacher is temporary and local, whilst the success will be permanent and world-wide. And thus, soberly reckoning with the facts of human nature as He had seen and felt them, and with the faithfulness of the Father who would yet make His work to prosper, He speaks His last words to the multitudes.

It scarcely falls within our present scope to treat the post-resurrection ministry of the Lord Jesus, but it has qualities which entirely separate it from the ministry He had hitherto fulfilled.

It is not the old superstitious, ghost-seeing fishermen of the Galilean storm who have put into the mouth of an apparition the words ascribed to our Lord at His successive manifestations. As an able theological writer has justly observed, the spirits of the unjustly slain speak a very different language when they are supposed to visit the scenes of their past wrongs. Jesus does not come back crying out against His adversaries, or seeking to put right this portentous miscarriage of justice. His speech is coloured by two things, the fact that He has to build up the faith and courage of the disciples who have learned to love Him, but whose real work is only about to begin; and the fact that, since He died upon the cross, although He is still the same sympathetic Son of Man, a new sense of power, authority, victorious strength, everlasting salvation, has impressed itself upon His spirit. "Peace be unto you." "Receive ye the Holy Ghost." "All authority has been given unto Me in heaven and on earth. Go ye therefore and make disciples of all the nations." A new environment has come down out of heaven to compass Him on every side, and He is now responding to the stimulations inherent in a nobler circle of life and destiny.

MORRISON AND GIBB, PRINTERS, EDINBURGH

"The editor of this series of Handbooks is to be heartily congratulated. He has chosen his subjects well, and he has chosen the right men for them."—*The Expository Times.*

BOOKS FOR BIBLE STUDENTS.
Editor: Rev. ARTHUR E. GREGORY.

THE SWEET SINGER OF ISRAEL. Selected Psalms, illustrative of David's Character and History, with Metrical Paraphrases. By BENJAMIN GREGORY, D.D. 2s. 6d.

"It contains some excellent specimens of the best kind of devotional commenting. Of parade of scholarship there is none; of its patience and accuracy, evidences are to be found on almost every page. The charm of the paraphrases increases as the reader recognises more clearly, each time of reading, their high quality as poetry, and their adequacy as an exhibition of David's actual thoughts. But it is in the devotional commenting that the excellence of the book especially lies. Illustrations from a wide range of literature and from an intimate acquaintance with human nature play about the passages, bringing out the truthfulness to life of their teaching, and its serviceableness to the soul. It is a choice book, fresh, rich, vigorous, 'honey out of the rock' served up with 'the fat of the wheat'; and its venerable author could hardly better crown his great services to the Churches than by giving them more."—Professor Moss in *The Preacher's Magazine.*

THE PRAISES OF ISRAEL: An Introduction to the Study of the Psalms. By W. T. DAVISON, M.A., D.D. *Third Thousand.* 2s. 6d.

Dr. MARCUS DODS writes: "As nearly perfect as a manual can be. It is the work of a reverent and open-minded scholar, who has spared no pains to compress into this small volume the best information and the most trustworthy results arrived at by himself and other experts."

"It gives all that is most required and most apposite in an Introduction to the Study of the Psalms. It gives this in admirable form; everywhere it furnishes the results of the best scholarship without the parade of learning."—*Critical Review.*

THE WISDOM LITERATURE OF THE OLD TESTAMENT. By W. T. DAVISON, M.A., D.D. *Second Thousand.* 2s. 6d.

"Dr. Davison has followed up his attractive volume on *The Praises of Israel* by another equally attractive. These are amongst the best contributions to the series."—*Critical Review.*

"It will take its place among those modern 'Helps' to the interpretation of Scripture which place the English reader almost on a level with those who can read the Bible in its original languages."—*Methodist Times.*

FROM MALACHI TO MATTHEW: Outlines of the History of Judea from 440 to 4 B.C. By Professor R. WADDY MOSS. *Second Thousand.* 2s. 6d.

"Mr. Moss's book is worthy of the series. His style is straightforward and graphic. He can tell a story rapidly and forcibly. There is vigour and there is vitality throughout. It is to be hoped that these manuals will be largely used."—*The British Weekly.*

BOOKS FOR BIBLE STUDENTS—*Continued.*

AN INTRODUCTION TO THE STUDY OF HEBREW.
By J. T. L. MAGGS, B.A., Prizeman in Hebrew and New Testament Greek, London University. Small crown 8vo, 5s.

Rev. W. F. MOULTON, D.D., says: "I do not know any book within the same compass which approaches this in usefulness for the beginner. The Reading Lessons, fully annotated and supplied with references to the sections of the grammar, will prove of great service. I heartily congratulate the editor of the series on securing the aid of so able and scholarly a writer."

Canon DRIVER says: "Would prove to be well adapted for the class of students whose needs it is designed to meet."

IN THE APOSTOLIC AGE: The Churches and the Doctrine.
By R. A. WATSON, M.A., D.D. 2s. 6d.

"Well fitted to be used as a text-book. . . . Every reader will be thankful for so vigorous, fresh, and candid a treatment of the most important period of the life of Church and doctrine."—*The Expositor.*

"Certainly one of the ablest books in the series. Dr. Watson is a powerful and courageous thinker, furnished with competent scholarship and knowledge. The book addresses itself to the Bible student, and directs his attention to matters that require to be noted at the outset of his studies in Church History. Its method is as instructive as its substance."—*Wesleyan Methodist Magazine.*

THE GOSPEL OF ST. JOHN: An Exposition, with Short Notes.
By THOS. F. LOCKYER, B.A. *Second Thousand.* 2s. 6d.

"A terse, fresh, and thoughtful exposition of the Gospel of John. Every preacher will find useful hints in it, and the price is amazingly low—over three hundred pages for half-a-crown. It deserves to have a wide circulation."—*The British Weekly.*

THE EPISTLES OF PAUL THE APOSTLE: A Sketch of their Origin and Contents.
By GEORGE G. FINDLAY, B.A. *Fifth Thousand.* 2s. 6d.

"The reader will find here compressed into a small space what he must otherwise seek through many volumes. . . . Mr. Findlay has before now proved himself an able and accomplished expositor of St. Paul, and this little work will fully maintain his character."—*The Scotsman.*

THE THEOLOGICAL STUDENT: A Handbook of Elementary Theology.
By J. ROBINSON GREGORY. *Fifth Thousand.* 2s. 6d.

An Explanatory Index of Theological Terms and a very full list of Questions for Self-Examination add greatly to the practical value of the book.

"Mr. Gregory is . . . a born and trained theologian. Some departments he has made well-nigh his own—especially the doctrine of the Last Things. And better than that, he can write for beginners."—*The Expository Times.*

BOOKS FOR BIBLE STUDENTS—Continued.

THE AGE AND AUTHORSHIP OF THE PENTATEUCH. By WILLIAM SPIERS, M.A., F.G.S. Small crown 8vo, 3s. 6d.

"At once popular in style and scholarly in substance. It is up to date both in science and literature, yet faithful to the Word of God. Of all the 'Books for Bible Students' yet edited by Mr. Gregory, none are more needed or should be more welcomed than this. We trust it may be widely read."—*Sword and Trowel.*

"Gives a full survey of the argument in defence, and has been carefully prepared."—*Expositor.*

A MANUAL OF MODERN CHURCH HISTORY. By W. F. SLATER, M.A. 2s. 6d.

"This is a rare half-crown's worth. It ought to be eagerly bought up till edition after edition is exhausted. It is difficult to lay down this quintessence of Modern Church History when once we have taken it up. It is every way so good. The style is clearness itself. Nor is it devoid of pithy and poetic phrase. A more luminous history none could wish to read."—*Methodist Times.*

AN INTRODUCTION TO THE STUDY OF NEW TESTAMENT GREEK. By J. HOPE MOULTON, M.A., late Fellow of King's College Cambridge, and Master in the Leys School. 3s.

THE BOOKS OF THE PROPHETS. By GEORGE G. FINDLAY, B.A. Vol. I. To the Fall of Samaria. 2s. 6d.

THE MINISTRY OF THE LORD JESUS. By T. G. SELBY, Author of "The Imperfect Angel," etc. 2s. 6d.

THE DIVINE PARABLE OF HISTORY: An Exposition of the Revelation of St. John. By HENRY ARTHUR SMITH, M.A. 2s. 6d.

A FIRST READER IN NEW TESTAMENT GREEK. By J. HOPE MOULTON, M.A. [*In the Press.*

THE LAY PREACHER'S HANDBOOK; First Steps in Homiletics. By Rev. C. O. ELDRIDGE, B.A., with Preface by Rev. ARTHUR E. GREGORY. *Third Thousand.* Small crown 8vo, 2s.

"'Beauty for Ashes' would describe the change which would come to some pulpits, if only the men who preach would take to heart the instructions given in this book."—*Joyful News.*

"Written with care, ease, and simplicity, and is just the book we should like to see in the hands of all young men beginning to preach."—*Preacher's Magazine.*

"Admirably adapted to the needs of our own local preachers. . . . The book does not consist of pious platitudes; from beginning to end it is practical and sensible."—*Methodist Recorder.*

"Clear, sensible, practical."—*North British Daily Mail.*

London: **CHARLES H. KELLY, 2, Castle St., City Road, E.C.** and **66, Paternoster Row, E.C.**

"*The Preacher's Magazine* maintains its place as the first of the homiletic monthlies, and the rest are not in sight."—*Expository Times.*

The Preacher's Magazine.

FOR PREACHERS, TEACHERS, AND BIBLE STUDENTS.

PRICE FOURPENCE MONTHLY.

Editors: MARK GUY PEARSE and ARTHUR E. GREGORY.

Amongst the Contributors are

The Very Rev. C. J. Vaughan, D.D.
Ven. Archdeacon Farrar, D.D.
W. Hay M. H. Aitken, M.A.
Professor J. Agar Beet, D.D.
David Brook, M.A., B.C.L.
Archibald G. Brown.
John Clifford, D.D.
William Cuff.
W. H. Dallinger, LL.D., F.R.S.
W. T. Davison, D.D.
W. J. Dawson.
Professor G. G. Findlay, B.A.
Charles Garrett.
Professor A. S. Geden, M.A.
J. Monro Gibson, D.D.
Benjamin Gregory, D.D.
F. Harper, M.A.
R. F. Horton, D.D.
H. P. Hughes, M.A.

Charles Leach, D.D.
J. Scott Lidgett, M.A.
J. T. L. Maggs, B.A.
Professor R. Waddy Moss.
J. Hope Moulton, M.A.
Charles New.
Joseph Parker, D.D.
T. G. Selby.
W. Spiers, M.A., F.G.S.
Professor W. F. Slater, M.A.
H. Arthur Smith, M.A.
James Stalker, D.D.
Professor G. T. Stokes, D.D.
T. Bowman Stephenson, LL.D.
Professor J. G. Tasker.
Principal T. Vincent Tymms.
R. A. Watson, D.D.
W. L. Watkinson.

OPINIONS OF THE PRESS, ETC.

Mr. Spurgeon: "As good as the *very best* of its homiletical compeers. It goes in for practical suggestion, which will be really useful to men labouring to save souls. We like such magazines, and feel helped by looking them through. Each number is a capital return for the money."

Professor J. A. Beet, D.D.: "This is a thoroughly good magazine. From end to end it is full of first-rate homiletic matter."

Dr. Charles Parkhurst (New York): "It is the best help of the kind I have seen for many a day."

Thomas Champness: "We especially recommend the younger men to buy this magazine. These are days when pulpit freshness is in demand, and we do well to read that which will suggest ideas we have not thought of, and which will strike our hearers by its freedom from mildew."

The Christian Leader: "A periodical of very high tone and wide sphere of usefulness. It has specially helpful notes and illustrations. . . . A brilliant monthly."

The Methodist Sunday School Record: "The very best thing we have seen in the way of suggestiveness for workers, preachers, and teachers for Children's Sunday is furnished in the *Preacher's Magazine.*"

Sent Post Free for Twelve Months for 4s.

Specimen Copy post free for Fourpence.

London: C. H. KELLY, 2, Castle Street, City Road, E.C.;
AND 66, Paternoster Row, E.C.

www.ingramcontent.com/pod-product-compliance
Lightning Source LLC
Chambersburg PA
CBHW030013240426
43672CB00007B/932